DEMAIN PUBLISHING

Short Sharp Shocks!

Murder! Mystery! Mayhem!

Beats! Ballads! Blank Verse!

Weird! Wonderful! Other Worlds

Horror Novels & Novellas

Science Fiction Novels & Novellas

The 'A QUIET APOCALYPSE' Series

General Fiction

Science Fiction Collections

Horror Fiction Collections

Anthologies

Audios

BEING FOLLOWED
BY
DEREK MUK

Publisher's Note:
In the work that follows the Author's original American English spelling/intention has been retained.

I want to thank my beta readers, Kelly Gorman, Matt Schwartz, and Ana Brazil for reviewing the book. And I also want to thank Thomas Cooney for professionally editing the manuscript.

- <u>Derek Muk, January 2024</u>

CONTENTS

CHAPTER ONE

Albert Taylor hated being sick; hated it more than anything else.

Suddenly, the startling and persistent shrill of his cell phone's ringtone prodded him into motion, and he sluggishly reached over to the nightstand until his hand made contact with the device. He coughed before snatching up the phone and looking at the caller ID on the screen.

Claire

That single name rattled him back to a different place and time. A time when he was a different man. A younger man. Though it was a happier and simpler time, it roused up a whole slew of other emotions as well.

Oh, Claire, he thought. That name made him pause for a brief moment and he was immediately jerked back into 1995, New York City, Columbia University, and the Upper West Side. Other locales popped up in his head as well: Central Park, Greenwich Village, Times Square.

He tapped the 'answer' button and lifted the phone up to his ear.

He coughed again, wiping phlegm from his mouth with some tissue paper, before saying softly and hoarsely, "Claire."

"Oh Lord, that cough is as nasty and as vicious as it sounds!" she replied.

"It's a bear all right," he said, before erupting into another series of coughing fits again. "Actually, much worse." He paused to take a couple of weak, labored breaths before continuing. "I liken it more to the bubonic plague or some apocalyptic virus."

"Oh, dear!" she said. "Poor Albert! What's your temperature now?"

"104."

"You saw your doctor?"

"Yes."

"I made you some soup. Lemme bring it over."

"No!" he protested. "And get you sick as well?"

"Oh, don't worry, I'm going to take every universal health precaution, believe me. See you soon."

Before he could argue the point any further Claire had already hung up the phone. He coughed again, sighing in frustration. *Ex-wives. They were more stubborn than when they were still married.*

* * *

Claire's magic chicken soup did the trick. She must've followed some sacred and holy recipe to the letter because by week's end his fever, coughing spells, muscle aches, and night chills were gone. God bless her! The super woman cured his flu! The following Monday he was back at work, functioning normally again. All thanks to her.

When they got together after work that day, at his house, she fessed up.

"So what kind of special mushrooms did you put in that chicken soup?" he asked.

Her big brown eyes suddenly played all innocent and naïve with him, harkening back to those hush-hush, whisper, whisper days of youth so long ago. "You really want to know?"

"Do tell, please."

"It's my mother's secret recipe." Those eyes of hers searched for signs of recognition in his face, testing his memory. "Don't you remember?"

And just like that, a synapse flared in his brain, triggering his recall, and it all came back to him, pouring out of the flood gates like a caged beast. He nodded. "Oh, yeah! Her magic recipe. It was delicious as always."

Claire smiled. "Thank you. I'll pass the compliment on to her."

"Please do. And give her my warmest regards as well."

"I shall." She tilted her head a little like she always did when she was checking in with him. "So, you're feeling better now. Everything else okay?"

"Yes."

She paused for a moment, looking briefly at the surface of the coffee table, before saying, "You're probably wondering why I was so vague on the phone earlier."

"What's on your mind?" he prodded gently.

When Claire hesitated, Albert gently reached over and took her warm hand, with its soft and smooth skin, squeezing it tenderly. "Tell me," he said. They had engaged in numerous deep conversations since the divorce and had committed to the oath of remaining the best of friends. In his mind this shouldn't be any different. She could talk to him about anything.

"It's this," she replied. That absolute still and precise tone in her voice when she said it, one of being unnerved and scared out of her wits. She fished an envelope out of her purse. Not a white standard, business-sized one but more like one that would carry a greeting card.

She had said it with an edge of dread in her voice, as if the envelope were the plague itself or utter and complete filth and didn't want to ever lay a finger on it ever again for as long as she lived.

He took the envelope from her, opened it, and gingerly removed a single sheet of white paper from it. After unfolding the letter, he read it once and then a second time.

Maybe it was because of the content of the letter that it almost slipped from his hands but he managed to catch it before it dropped to the ground. Flipping the sheet over, he frowned as he studied the black lettered words once more, typed by using standard Microsoft Word by the looks of it (he'd read enough student papers in his academic career to make this observation.): **'If you release that book you will pay with your life, you kike bitch!'**

He looked at the hostile and nasty words once more before quickly grabbing a nearby Kleenex tissue to carefully pick up the envelope and turn it over to its other side. No return address, as he expected.

"I'll have the police analyze this," he said, before turning his attention back to her. "When did you get it?"

She shivered a little as she stared at the letter. "Few days ago."

"Do you know who could've sent it?"

Claire pushed her glasses up her nose before answering. "Let me backtrack and preface it by saying that the note is in reference to a manuscript that I had been working on for a while, concerning my research and study of the white nationalist movement which includes profiles of controversial think tank groups such as Utopia Euro-West and Blitzkrieg Blood Reich."

"So, it's an *exposé*?"

Being a native New Yorker, she quickly utilized her New York second in defense of her work. "Well, I wouldn't describe it that generically...uhmmm, I think the book fits within the scope of what I envisioned it to be from the very beginning, the moment of its conception, as an academic research book on the rising tide of this movement and the harmful and quite dangerous side effects and consequences it has on society. An extremely important project, I believe, that everyone should read and be aware of." Touting and tooting her horn proudly, showcasing her saleswoman skills and prowess unabashedly, which she frequently did for she was one who wasn't afraid to speak her mind, especially when it pertained to issues she felt very passionate about. That was his Claire, all right, to the T. And something that he really loved about her and wouldn't want her to change, ever. Nothing like a strong, independent woman who had an opinion on everything, and who also had an edge and a backbone and who cared about important social issues such as this. In his book that was very sexy indeed.

"Gotcha," he replied. "I want to read it." Pitching in his two cents and lending his support.

Claire smiled at him. "Happy to know I've got you as a supporter in my corner."

"Always. The book is available now?"

She nodded. "Has been for two weeks. I'm *not* going to live in fear and let these creeps scare me and run my life for me...you can go ahead and feel free and take your pick of enemies from the litter box. Wide open field here, mister, anyone from Utopia Euro-West on down. Basically, that includes any individuals who don't like my views." Claire counted a few things with the fingers on her right hand, letting each finger flip out like a blade from a switchblade. "Be it anti-feminists, anti-Semites, anti-progressives, anti-liberals."

"Hmmm. Have you received any other threats besides this letter?"

She nodded at the paper, a strained expression on her face. "Isn't that enough?"

"Any students or faculty who don't appreciate your opinions?"

"There are some from those camps." She looked away quietly. "But hardly enough with the motivation to carry out a scheme such as this I think."

"Everyone's a suspect at this point as far as I'm concerned," he replied solemnly.

***

September 1995, Columbia University, New York City

Claire thought the humidity would literally melt her down to the famous Low Steps. *Seriously.* It was that severe, probably one of the hottest and stickiest summers on record in the Big Apple as far as she could recall. And then she'd be nothing but a foul-smelling puddle of flesh and bones awaiting poor Albert. True, she didn't know him from Adam, they'd only recently met, but he deserved better than that, much better. And he seemed like a nice enough guy, maybe a bit shy and quiet, at least from what she observed so far, but that was fine. She was like that sometimes.

While she waited under that sweltering afternoon sun, reclining on the steps with her headphones blasting Lou Reed's "Perfect Day" into her ears she took a gander at the festive sights around her: numerous little clusters of students, some of which included fellow classmates that she recognized, sat huddled together on the steps around her, chatting away incessantly about this and that, giggling, laughing until their tummies hurt and their faces were cherry red. Some acting totally silly, some rowdy and boisterous like they were at the campus pub. And they were gathered here due in large part because of the nice if extreme weather conditions. For her, part of her ultimate college fantasy was to recline on these legendary steps and just take in the scene, the atmosphere and the ambiance, and just chill. Because classes were tough and stressful as it were, expectations sky high, not to mention school tuition. So it was perfectly fine, from time to time (though not too often), to just take it easy and zone out. And what a day to do so, to just sit under that sun and soak in the rays.

As the song slowly reached its conclusion, a set of slightly damp hands suddenly clamped around her eyes from behind.

"Guess who?" a male voice asked.

"Phil Simms!" she blurted out, for those strong and rugged hands injected her with a flight of fancy, making her imagine the quarterback of the New York Giants.

"I wish!" the voice answered. "How I wish I could throw a perfect spiral and live a charmed and glamorous life as a famous athlete. But no, I'm just a lowly student."

"At Columbia!" she giggled, turning around to face a young, dark-haired man with just a touch of acne, and sporting the biggest and nerdiest pair of glasses she'd seen since the 1980s, ones with a generic silver frame that were all the rage back then. His face was slick with perspiration.

"How you doing?" he asked, sitting next to her on the steps.

She removed her headphones, stashing them away in her backpack along with her battered but trusty Walkman. "Aside from this heat, just brilliant. Now coming from a native New Yorker, born and bred here, to show you how hot it is exactly, just touch my skin, would ya please, Albert?"

He did as instructed, touching her forearm gently.

"Feel how warm it is?" Claire asked, looking at him for confirmation to validate her point.

"Uhhh, yes, it is indeed. The effects of the sun."

"Boy oh boy!" she replied. "Is it ever! I bet it never gets this humid and hot out in Cali. Didn't you say that's where you're from?"

"Correct. No, you're right. We don't have the extreme weather like you do here. Though I have to admit I love seeing the snow out here and the changing of the seasons!" He smiled. "That's cool!"

"Betcha you wouldn't appreciate shoveling out snow from a driveway in the winter, though," she countered. "You don't have to deal with that way out in Cali. Lucky sons of guns." She tilted her head philosophically and looked at him when she made the remark.

"Not unless you go to the mountains in the winter," he said, meeting her gaze.

Claire suddenly beamed and blurted, "But enough trivial talk about the weather! Why do strangers *always, always* wind up chatting about the frickin' weather? You asked for a grand tour of the city and I'm here to grant your request, or at least a part one of it, if you will, for this place is huge."

"Tell me about it!"

She zipped up her backpack, slinging it on. "So, now that our classes are done for today, lemme take you over to Central Park for starters since it's not that far from here. 'Cause everybody falls in love with New York, especially the park. I think you'll like it. Then I thought, if time permits,

I'll show you where you can grab a real yummy New York hot dog. Or a slice of a real New York City pizza if you fancy that instead. How does that sound?"

Albert grinned at her. "Sounds great!"

And off they went on their grand adventure of the Big Apple, or to a small part of it at least.

CHAPTER TWO

Albert kept checking the time on his phone, nervously pacing in circles at Gate 22 where the new international exchange students from Hong Kong were due to arrive at any minute. He had hosted exchange students at his house before so he didn't know exactly where his anxiety stemmed from this time around. Maybe it was just jitters about having strangers staying at his home again, his sanctuary, his refuge away from the wilds of civilization. That was totally understandable for he'd heard his fair share of horror stories concerning colleagues of his who had students living with them in the past. But fortunately those kind of nightmarish situations were rare. He'd never had a negative experience hosting students. Besides, these two students who were coming really seemed like nice people. From what he gleaned and observed from their numerous phone conversations, video conferences, and email messages, they seemed like genuinely hardworking and studious people who had the grades and academic background to prove it. Plus the fact that they passed the criminal background check and other standard security protocols. No weird behaviors, strange posts, or crazy rants on social media, either. He checked.

Then why was he still anxious? That pestering and annoying thing that was still festering in the back part of his mind. *New encounters like this...it's totally natural*, he kept telling himself. Nothing strange about it.

Accompanying him on this journey was a young, slender woman named Jan who had red shoulder length hair, and who kept scribbling away every so often in a ubiquitous journal of hers that she carried around everywhere. Be it on campus, off campus, on investigations, at research digs, at the local grocery store, and at all the student cafes. He literally couldn't recall a time when she was actually without it. That was kind of scary. Well, there were worse things than that, he supposed. At least she wasn't staring at her phone all the time.

He leaned against a pillar at the gate, watching her for a second, wondering what the hell she was writing about. What could be so pressing and fascinating to her that she would remain transfixed with her eyes glued to the page? Almost to the point of being oblivious to others and her surroundings. That was also scary. But who was he to judge?

He decided a little distraction was in order, shooting her a sly grin and asking, "Whatcha writing, scribe?" His apt, little nickname for her.

Jan immediately looked up from her journal, noticing him for the very first time it seemed, a sheepish expression on her face. "Huh?"

Albert maintained his smile. "Never mind. Carry on, scribe. I'll just continue talking to myself, or maybe to that chair over there."

She shut her journal, stuffing it in her backpack without hesitation. "Oh, I'm sorry, Teach!" Her apt, little nickname for him. "I just got lost in my own little world again. Sorry! Happens to the best of us, you know."

He almost replied back by saying: 'But it always happens with you.' But he refrained. Instead, he checked the time on his phone again, glad he wasn't pacing around in circles anymore. He caught some folks staring at him for doing that, probably because he was making them nervous. Things always seemed to have a way of rubbing off on folks.

Instead, he started to say: "They should be—"

But she interrupted him, beating him to the punch, by pointing towards the large, panoramic windows, where they saw a Boeing 747 with the United Airlines logo on it, pulling itself up to the gate.

"It's here!" she said with a bit of excitement evident in her voice as if the circus was back in town.

"Well, I'll be darned," he replied, putting his phone away. "It's about time!"

They waited patiently along with the other people at the gate as the process of disembarking began. Minutes later, after a flurry of folks hurried past them, Albert finally recognized a pair of familiar faces in the sea of humanity and waved enthusiastically at them.

"Hey, over here!" he said. When they got closer, he shook their hands and added: "Hi, Lee. Hello, Pei. Welcome to San Francisco!"

"Thank you!" Lee, a young man, replied, traces of a British Hong Kong accent in his voice. "Glad to finally be able to meet you."

"Likewise," Albert said. "Boy, those were a lot of phone calls and emails we exchanged, huh?"

Pei, a young woman with her hair tied back in a ponytail, laughed. "Yes, they were. But they were good talks. It has been nice chatting with you."

Albert grinned. "I agree. I enjoyed them as well." He gestured to the red-haired woman. "This is my graduate teaching assistant, Jan. Jan, this is Lee and Pei. They are going to be staying with me for the academic year."

Jan smiled and shook hands with the two. "Pleasure meeting the both of you. I've heard so many good things about you and look forward to working with you. I hope you enjoy your time in the Bay Area."

"Thank you," the two exchange students replied, almost simultaneously.

Jan nodded at their suitcases. "Can I help you with your luggage?"

"No, we got it," Pei answered. "Thank you. Actually, there's more!"

"Oh, the baggage claim area!" Albert interjected, as if suddenly remembering a very important plot detail in a movie. "We'd better get going before it gets to be a mob scene over there."

* * *

They returned to Albert's house across the bay, with the traffic heading east bound across the Bay Bridge surprisingly smooth and light for a change. Once they were in Berkeley proper, it was even smoother sailing going along University Avenue up to San Pablo Avenue. He made a left turn on San Pablo and they traversed the several blocks quite easily, making it back in record time.

The pair of exchange students quickly got situated in his medium-sized humble abode once a brief introduction was made as to where the basics were located: the bathroom, kitchen, and their bedrooms. While they were unpacking in their respective rooms, Albert sat down on the living room sofa and took the liberty of checking his text and voicemail messages on his phone. Jan, meanwhile, sat on the other end of the sofa, her face buried and preoccupied in that journal of hers again, with her pen furiously scribbling away on a fresh, blank slate of white paper. *She was at it again!* What was she chronicling for crying out loud? Her life story? The Great American Novel? In the ensuing silence he heard the swooshes and abrupt skid marks her pen made on paper.

He turned and looked at her. "How dramatic!" he remarked, trying his hand at sarcastic humor.

Her response to that was pure and focused concentration, her brow furrowed as she poured her thoughts out on the page, as though she hadn't heard him at all. That's probably how she was during her studies, with that poker study face, and she definitely had the grades to substantiate that. Ah, heck, he didn't mind one bit because Jan came and hung out at his place quite often. She commented once that his house was a nice escape, a nice diversion, from the usual locales to study such as the library, the café, and her own apartment. Actually, *lounge*, was the more correct word to describe her body posture when she came over to study or work. She'd lie back on a cushion or pillow on this very couch, prop her feet up on the coffee table or the arm of the sofa, and just read away or immerse herself in work on her laptop, or better yet, her journal.

"Would you like a cup of coffee and Danish, Miss?" he asked, making another casual attempt at humor again.

Her reaction this time around was more receptive as she actually looked up from her journal, beaming ear-to-ear at him. "Awwwww, that's so sweet of you. Sure! Is that Danish gluten free?"

He guffawed, shattering the peaceful tranquility of the living room. "You youngsters ruined the good, old-fashioned purity of food with that crap! Now everything has to be that way or has to be organic or trans fat-free." Which made him think of Claire all of a sudden for she had adopted and adhered to such a lifestyle. *Vegetarian.* Well, not quite that extreme but still, she had been practicing it for a while now. Goody, goody for her. Maybe that healthy code of living of hers would rub off on him. Lord knew he surely needed it. That soup she made for him was certainly yummy and nourishing. He'd love to have more of that and whatever else she concocted. He missed her cooking, among other things, and longed for the spices, seasonings, and aromas that wafted from the kitchen when she was busy puttering around in it. That made him smile. Claire made him smile.

"I'd like to live longer, Teach, that's why," Jan explained, taking a break from her writing.

"Yeah, yeah, yeah," he said, putting his phone away.

Pei came into the living room seconds later, a look of complete innocence on her face, as she caught the tail end of the conversation. "Did you mention food?" she asked shyly.

"Yes," Albert replied. "You hungry?"

Pei nodded immediately, grinning. Lee joined them moments later, hands casually parked in the front pockets of his jeans.

"Well, if I had fresh food in the house, I'd cook you all a nice meal," Albert began. "But since that's not the case how about I take you out for dinner? What kind of food do you like?"

"You pick since you are the host and we are the guests in your home," Pei answered, her voice having that same distinctive British Hong Kong accent like Lee's.

Albert thought for a moment. "Do you like pho?"

Pei nodded. "Oh, yes! That's fine."

Lee nodded in agreement.

"Great!" Albert said, getting up from the sofa. "Let's go."

CHAPTER THREE

"It's a dialogue about how white nationalism threatens the very fabric of not just multiculturalism but of feminism as well," Claire said, proudly raising the book that she penned, as she stood in front of the mostly full classroom, with the majority of the students being female. "White nationalism rips apart the core basics and fundamentals of our society, as well as everything progressives and liberals have built and secured, and not just for the past and current generations but for the future ones as well. White supremacist ideals and concepts did not perish completely in Nazi Germany at the end of World War II after the slaughter of so many Jews and so-called undesirables, as many have thought. On the contrary, the many seeds the Nazi party planted back then have sprouted all over this nation, as well as this entire world, infecting and poisoning the minds of our youth. It's a giant corporation, an evil empire, that's hell bent on recruiting and collecting as many young souls it possibly can without care or regard as to the safety and well-being of others. The rising tide of white nationalism is at an all-time high now, as statistics in my book clearly illustrate. They are literally at our front doorstep, folks."

She paused for a moment, making eye contact with each student, letting this important information sink in, before adding, "Your homework assignment for this week is to read chapters three, four, and five and write a paper about how white nationalism has affected your own experiences, your own views, as a woman, man, transgender person, gay, lesbian, bisexual, or any other affiliation that you identify with. If you have any questions please ask me...okay, that's it. Thank you and have a great week, everyone." Then Claire suddenly remembered something and quickly darted back to the chalkboard to write the following down: **My office hours are Mondays and Wednesdays, 4pm-5pm, and Fridays from 3pm to 4pm.**

And added her office phone number and email address to the chalkboard for good measure even though it was already listed on the class syllabus. People always forgot things or were too lazy to look them up sometimes. A few of her students jotted down the information before leaving the classroom.

After another student left, she grew more and more aware of the encroaching silence and of the eerie ticking sound of the wall clock, as if the wax had been cleared from her ears and her hearing was super enhanced and acute now. Quite frankly, the sensation was driving her crazy and she couldn't wait to get out of here. It was just her and a few people now, who were either checking their phones or were slowly loading their books, notepads, and pens into their backpacks before zipping them up.

Claire was busy gathering her own personal items as well at the front of the classroom, tossing them into a bag. After pushing her glasses up her nose and making a few additional notations on her pad she capped her pen, grabbed her phone, and prepared to leave.

Two students got up and made their way to the door, stepping out before her. She was the last one to exit, turning the lights off. Good habit of hers, always the energy saver.

In the hallway outside, one of those students, a mousy looking woman with wide and timid eyes, asked her, "Say, are you going towards the parking garage?"

"Yes I am," Claire replied.

"Mind if I walk with you?"

Claire smiled at her. "Not at all. I always enjoy a little company on walks."

The mousy looking woman seemed to ease up a bit and appeared more reassured but her wide eyes kept darting back and forth, as if on the constant lookout for potential predators. "The reason I asked is because about a week ago a woman got mugged and sexually assaulted on one of the trails leading to the garage."

Claire turned and stared at her. "Really?" How could she have missed out on such important news such as that? Well, very easily, unfortunately, by being sucked up and immersed in her own busy work world, much like anybody else.

Mavis, the mousy looking woman, nodded, her eyes maintaining their vigilance and alertness around them as they traversed down the length of a dimly lit gravel path. The skies above them were slowly growing darker. Sunset was approaching fast.

"Did they apprehend the attacker?" Claire asked, her boots making crunching noises on the gravel.

Mavis shook her head.

Claire frowned. "How unfortunate."

"I know," the woman said quietly.

They walked in silence for a bit, approaching a lone lamppost along the path and beyond that, the looming concrete monstrosity of the parking garage. Mavis immediately pointed to a flyer taped to the lamppost, which had a sketch of a bald white man on it.

"That's the suspect," Mavis explained.

Claire took out her phone and captured the image with it. Then they resumed their trek to the garage which was deserted and half empty at this hour, partially engulfed in semi-darkness. Not looking promising or optimistic at all.

Mavis turned to her and asked, "Can you walk me to my car? I can give you a lift to yours."

"Sure." Claire was about to add, 'Hopefully he's not brazen enough to attack those in pairs,' but bit her tongue for she didn't want to scare this poor woman out of her wits any more than she already was. The poor woman's eyes told it all.

Minutes later, they reached Mavis' vehicle safely, got in, and drove off in search of Claire's own car on the fourth level. They found the vintage steel and chrome Mercedes Benz convertible from 1984. She sighed in relief and felt her eyes get watery upon seeing that ancient behemoth, of seeing a familiar object of hers that was like an old, trusted friend. They'd been through a lot together.

That car was a treasure trove of memories. And knowing that she'd soon be in it and zooming away from potential danger brought her much elation.

"Thanks again for escorting me," Mavis said quietly.

"You're welcome," Claire replied, injecting as much reassurance and confidence in her response as she could, hoping it would boost her mood. When she turned her head in the direction of her car again, and before she had even opened the passenger side door of this woman's vehicle, she noticed a small white object clipped under one of her car's windshield wipers, feeling a huge lump in her throat that prevented her from swallowing saliva, that prohibited her from breathing for a moment, that made her heart pound super-fast inside her chest like a jackhammer, for she already knew what that white object was before she even stepped out of the vehicle.

Oh, God, not again! Claire thought, trying to fight that feeling of dread and fear, that sudden stomach ache that came out of nowhere. Her stomach felt like it was being tied into multiple knots. She began coughing uncontrollably.

Mavis took notice of this, brow furrowing. "Are you okay?"

Claire fought back with all her might and will power, trying to suppress and smother that coughing fit that threatened to dominant and break her. *But* she was stronger, and after wrestling a bit with that inner force that was inside of her, Claire came out as the victor, taking a couple of deep breaths. She nodded slowly.

Claire climbed out of the woman's vehicle with her bag. Before shutting the door behind her, she said to the woman, "Thanks. I'll see you in class this Friday."

"See you Friday." Mavis waited and watched as Claire got safely in her own car and locked the doors before driving off. Before getting in, however, and using a Kleenex tissue to shield her hand, Claire gingerly removed the white business-sized envelope from under the windshield wiper, trying not to smudge any existing fingerprints that might already be on it.

Sitting in the dark, silent confines of her Mercedes convertible, still feeling the pangs of that stomach ache that was brought on by stress, fear, and anxiety, she stared with her mouth hanging open at that white envelope that sat in the passenger side seat as if it were a live scorpion or tarantula. *I'd better call Albert now and let him know.* She quickly fished her phone out of her purse and found his number. Her finger hovered over the **Call** button for a moment, and as she hesitated, her curiosity bit her and got a hold of her for she found her eyes darting back to that damn envelope on the passenger seat, being distracted by it. Big time! She was drawn to it like a magnet and she found herself being hypnotized by it and momentarily felt powerless, paralyzed even, to resist its effects on her. She tried to shake off its influence on her but only felt herself being sucked in by it more and more.

Claire found herself reaching over to grab that envelope, carefully opening it with the protection of the tissue paper, and unfolding the single sheet of 20lb white bond paper in the very same manner. She took a deep breath before reading the only line that was typed on that sheet. Same font, color, and size. Microsoft Word again, it appeared.

It read: **You're gonna die, you kike bitch, for disobeying us.**

CHAPTER FOUR

September 1995, Central Park Zoo, New York City

Claire lowered her hand, cupped full of animal food, next to the goat and it took the food from her hand. After nibbling on the initial offering the goat, not as shy and modest the second time around when she lowered her hand again, lowered its head once more and helped itself to some more grains which it chewed more heartily.

"*Awwwwww*, you're so cute," she said, petting the goat. "I'd love to take you home with me but you're so stinky!"

Albert chuckled.

"You need a bath!" she added. *"Like seriously!"*

The goat stopped chewing abruptly and stared up at her with that 'deer in the headlights, lost in love' kind of expression on its face.

"*Oh*, I think he *likes* you," Albert remarked coolly, a facetious trace of jealousy in his voice.

Claire started laughing. "Well, it wouldn't be the first time. I had that kind of effect, that memorable first impression, on an animal the last time I came here with my parents. Another goat, not this one in particular obviously, was all goo-goo, ga-ga for me, practically salivating in my lap."

Albert busted out laughing. "Ooooooh, love at first sight!"

She petted the goat one last time, said, "See ya, my prince," got up, and they began walking away. But noticing this, the goat started pushing against the gate, even shoving against it forcefully and nudging its head on it, trying to open the gate, bleating at them, or at *her* specifically.

Claire immediately stopped, spun around on her heel, and looked at the animal, her jaw dropping open a little. The goat looked up at her with a dazed kind of expression on its face, making that distinctive "maa" sound at her.

Her smile was one of flattery and surprise, petting the goat's head again. "Oh, I'm so sorry, but we have to get going, my dear friend. We have a schedule to stick to, sights to see, and some pressing matters to attend to. Oh, please forgive us, my prince...until the next time that I return to the zoo, please do entertain the other ladies on my account, but remember, please behave yourself and don't be a player, would you?" She winked at the goat, which kept bleating and licking her hand. "One girl at a time, okay?" Petting its head once more. "They may not be as nice and understanding as me...okay, bye now!"

Albert looked over his shoulder as they walked towards the exit. "Awww, you're breaking his little heart! He's still gazing at you! He's smitten."

Their next stop was the elephant exhibit where they waited for close to half an hour before they witnessed their first sighting of a large but rather emaciated looking elephant that stepped out from behind a cluster of trees, reaching up with its trunk to snag a piece of tree bark and eat it.

"Aww, poor guy, why is he so shriveled up?" Claire frowned. "Hope they aren't abusing him."

"That thought crossed my mind, too," Albert replied, leaning his elbows on the railing.

They waited patiently for the other elephants to come out, but they never did, and so the two moved on to the lion exhibit where a similarly looking lion, surprisingly not as robust and well fed as Claire had expected or hoped for, sauntered out of its den and scanned the environment around him. It opened its mouth and took a big yawn, a rather showy and somewhat rehearsed one at that, appearing rather bored and lazy of the human spectators, before strolling around in its enclosure, like it was taking a casual walk in the park, taking in the sights and sounds of it before finally settling down next to a small pond.

"Photo op," Albert suggested.

Claire fished out her little point and shoot camera out of her backpack, aiming and zooming in carefully at the lion, before snapping a couple of shots. "Gotcha!"

One of the highlights of that day was their sighting of the legendary snow leopard, which had made all the headlines in the news and captured everyone's heart and attention in New York. Before the elusive animal had the chance to escape from the public's curious eye Claire zipped out her little camera, aimed it, and captured the animal on film.

"Gotcha!" she muttered again. "Ha, ha!"

"Hey, you're pretty handy with that thing."

"Okay, is your stomach ready for that famous and iconic New York hot dog now?" she asked.

"Absolutely!" he replied, tapping his tummy with his hands.

"All right, all right!" Claire said. "Follow my lead then, buddy! You're gonna be salivating when we're a block away from this joint, believe me, because the mouthwatering aroma lingers that far. And these hot dogs are that good!"

"Bring it on then!" he grinned. "I've heard so many stories about New York City hot dogs back on the West Coast, hearing that they're the stuff made of legend, that they're the be all and end all of hot dogs and all that. Okay, I'm ready now!" He clapped his hands together in eager anticipation.

Later, after devouring not one but two of those famous New York City hot dogs, Albert sat Indian-style on a blanket across from her on a patch of freshly cut grass in one corner of the park, beaming from ear-to-ear. He had that 'very-satisfied-with-my-meal' kind of look on his face, soaking in the rays of that sweltering and relentlessly brutal sun. The sun that seemed to have absolutely no mercy on these poor, pathetic humans on planet Earth. Lying and sitting on the grass all around them were other folks seeking refuge from the heat wave, some playing Frisbee, some throwing a football around, and some playing volleyball. The rhythmic and upbeat tempo of conga drums could be heard in the distance accompanied by the strong and pungent odor of marijuana, wafting in on a warm breeze.

Claire watched as beads of sweat trickled down his cheeks. Thank God they were in the shade otherwise it would've been completely unbearable. "You missed a spot," she remarked.

"I beg your pardon?"

"You've got a smidgen of ketchup on your chin," she giggled.

"Oh!" He quickly wiped it away with some tissue paper, rubbing his tummy and licking his lips. "Damn, those were great hot dogs! Hit the spot perfectly."

"See?" she replied with a smirk, lying on her back on the blanket, and staring up at the skies. Her socks and shoes off. "Told you so, Mr. Cali. Now you can say to all your friends that you've tried them."

He nodded. "How'd you ever manage to survive all these years in New York with this kind of humidity and the severe winters? I've got to hand it to you. You've got balls, woman!"

She continued gazing up at the sky philosophically. "As strange as it may sound, you get used to it. As a native New Yorker, it's in my blood, I guess you can say. My whole nutty family attests to that, too. We've all got thick skin and all have dealt reasonably well with being in extreme and weird situations."

"That's a good trait. Being resilient like that."

Suddenly, a spontaneous idea, among countless other ones, popped into her head, and she grinned like the Cheshire cat. "Hey, wanna go grab some sangria?" she asked, thinking of the Lou Reed song, "Perfect Day," and trying to do all the things mentioned in the tune.

"After having those hot dogs?" Albert asked, sitting there and soaking in the heat, allowing the suggestion to percolate in his head for a moment. He smiled back at her and replied, "Hey, that's not a bad recommendation, tour guide. Would be a great way to cool off and refresh ourselves from this humidity."

Claire sat up, put her socks and shoes back on, and mopped the perspiration from her face with the sleeve of her Lou Reed T-shirt. After collecting her blanket and the rest of her stuff they moved on. She took him to a charming, little café with musicians playing reggae in an outdoor patio area, not far from the entrance where they initially entered the park. They grabbed a table on the patio.

"I'll grab us a pitcher of sangria, tour guide," Albert said, getting up from his chair. "Want anything else?"

"Nah!" Claire replied, swaying and snapping her fingers to the groove of the music. "I'm good."

One of the reggae musicians, the bass player, shot her a flirtatious grin, checking her out from head to toe. Claire quickly averted her eyes.

Albert returned moments later with a pitcher and two glasses, pouring her a glass first.

He clinked her glass and said, "Cheers!"

"Cheers!" she replied, taking a swig, noticing that the bass player kept staring at her, giving her that mad-dog-in-love kind of look, and making her feel uncomfortable.

She drank more sangria, hoping that it would make her feel less anxious. A few couples got up and started dancing to the music.

Another impromptu idea came to her. "Hey, wanna dance?"

"Sure, tour guide," he answered. "I've liked all your other recommendations so far."

They stood up and moved over to the small square of smooth sandstone that served as the dance floor, where she exploded in active and creative free form dance expression, shaking her head, her shoulders, her hips, and her butt like no one was watching. She didn't care. She wanted to loosen up and shake off that net of school-related stress that had accumulated since the semester began and had threatened to smother her to death, and just have some good, old fun now. Albert, arched his eyebrows, taken aback a little by this it appeared, as if he was witnessing a historical milestone or achievement or the birth of some new and groundbreaking trend, smiled and nodded his head in an animated, gung-ho manner, encouraging her to continue strutting her stuff and show her moves. She liked his gesture and the fact that he was supporting her to keep it going. She'd been on dates where the guy was flat-out boring and dull, showing no initiation, motivation, and desire to want to do anything except talk about themselves and their accomplishments and exploits. So this was definitely a nice change for the better.

"Yeah, baby!" he reassured her. "Woo-hoo!"

Claire kept her body in motion, jumping around, bouncing around, gyrating in circles occasionally, and trying to maintain that creative flow of energy. She almost lost her balance a few times from all the hustle and bustle and Albert caught her fall each and every time, causing her to giggle in his arms.

It was during one of these moments when she was cradled securely in his arms that he lowered his head, leaning in close to her, and gave her a kiss. Totally not expecting this, or at least not expecting it so soon, Claire reciprocated by returning him an equally ardent kiss. Like a tennis match from that point on, he volleyed back, leaning in close to her moist and sticky face, nose to nose, to deliver another kiss to her. When she kissed him back his lips and mouth tasted like ketchup, mustard, and alcohol. What a creative combination!

And that was how that evening of their first date sort of ended, on a romantic and upbeat note. All throughout the day she kept thinking of Lou Reed's song, "Perfect Day", and how she was glad and happy to have spent it with Albert. It felt magical, dream-like, and she hated to use the word, "perfect", to describe it. It almost felt like it couldn't be real. Because nothing was ever perfect, was it?

On the leisurely stroll back to her apartment, with his arm snugly around her shoulders, the two of them staring up at the clear, black nighttime skies over Manhattan, not a cloud in sight, gazing at those stars like typical love birds who were in a total daze about one another. The air still hot, sticky, and heavy. Earthquake or tornado weather.

It was probably about seventy-five or seventy-six degrees now, easily.

Claire rolled her eyes and groaned, "*Gawd*, it's still so warm now that I can practically sleep out on the sidewalk tonight!"

Albert grinned. "Hey, that's another great idea, tour guide! I'll join you. Beats being stuck in a stuffy and cramped unit all by my lonesome. Why don't we go pick out a spot and camp out? Whaddya say?"

She laughed. "And get killed in the process? You Californians are too naïve about New York City. It ain't as safe and heavenly as it's depicted in the movies, buddy. Just last week some poor guy got jumped and robbed in the park with the crap beat out of him. And all for just five measly dollars!"

"Jesus! Okay, let's jettison that idea."

Minutes later, they finally arrived at her apartment building, an atmospheric and historical looking brownstone near the university. A few teenagers on skateboards zipped by them, almost knocking them over.

"*Ooooops, sorry!*" one of them yelled.

"Well, that's New York City for you," she said, turning to Albert. "You gotta look both ways wherever you go. I hope you enjoyed my little personal and private tour for you today."

"I did immensely," he smiled, squeezing her shoulder and kissing her passionately on the lips again. "Thank you very much. Hey, let's do a part two sometime. Can you show me another part of the city?"

Claire looked up at him with a big smile and replied, "Sure! When we're both not swamped with homework and papers. I'll check my schedule and get back to you."

"Okay...say, can I come up with you?" he asked, nodding at the building.

She looked directly in his eyes, locking with them, seeing the passion and lust in them and his inclination for something more than just mere kissing and making out. "Uhhh...not tonight, I'm afraid. I've got some stuff to take care of...rain check though, okay, buddy?"

He kissed her again. "Okay. Oh, my God, your mouth tastes so delicious!"

Another idea sparked in that overactive brain of hers. A myriad of ideas were always racing and spinning in her head all the time, all vying for her personal attention. She tilted her head a little, looking at him as if sizing him up, and asked curiously, "Hey, do you like Jewish cuisine? I'll make you a nice, home-made kosher meal sometime, okay?"

"That sounds fantastic! I'd certainly be down for that."

"Okay then! We've got a plan. Goodnight, Albert." And she reached up to him to give him one last kiss for the night before they parted ways.

"Goodnight."

She could still see the longing and yearning in his eyes before she turned away and headed for the front door.

* * *

The big black sedan followed Claire's Mercedes convertible at a discreet and inconspicuous pace, always allowing a couple of other cars or a few cars to fill the gap between them, to ensure it would not be detected. Up ahead a Honda Accord's bright yellow turn signal suddenly flickered and the driver of the black sedan allowed the Honda to squeeze itself into the lane. Now there were a total of five cars between the Mercedes and the black sedan, creating a nice and comfortable cushion and cover. But it would be best not to let another vehicle cut into this lane for fear of losing the convertible.

The black sedan made a left turn onto Grand Avenue, staying in the right-hand side lane, and cruising by the tranquil beauty of Lake Merritt on the right. The orange-purplish sunset skies, appearing like swirling ice cream flavors, cast a somewhat garish light on the terrain, magnifying and intensifying certain key spots around the body of water. Runners, roller bladers, and dog walkers all wore sunglasses to shield themselves from the unusual illumination. A canoe full of rowers glided smoothly in the opposite direction of the sedan.

Soon they hit rush hour traffic as vehicles that had flowed in from downtown Oakland clogged all of the lanes heading towards Interstate 580 as well as towards the Piedmont area. Fortunately, the Mercedes avoided the freeway, veered slightly right, and sped along Lakeshore Avenue until it signaled left and slowly pulled into a gated parking lot of a complex near the famous steps of the Cleveland Cascade. The driver of the black sedan quickly snagged an empty slot along the curb across from the building, turned to his left, and watched Claire get out of her car and step inside the complex.

He glanced at his watch and waited patiently, admiring the serene view of the lake for a moment as a few joggers trudged on by, before turning his attention back to the apartment building. Approximately fifteen minutes later, Claire exited the complex in a T-shirt, black shorts, and sneakers, and started running on a paved path along the lake, heading towards the old Henry J. Kaiser Convention Center and the Alameda County Courthouse. So far, it appeared that the driver was still under Claire's radar. He wanted to keep it that way and swiftly climbed out of the sedan, crossed the street to the apartment building, and quickly got to work.

CHAPTER FIVE

The young man with the peculiar hairstyle, short on the sides and long on top, stood on the stage facing the crowd that was growing larger by the minute. He scanned the faces in the audience, making a concentrated effort at eye contact with everyone, establishing that connection which was so critical and so vital in situations like this, and letting them know they were all in this important cause together. They were *not* in this situation by themselves. He saw one man proudly raising a sign that said: **I'M FOR A WHITER AMERICA. HOW ABOUT YOU, BROTHERS AND SISTERS?** A woman standing directly in front of the stage held up a poster board that read: **Please protect the white race, protect the white culture, and our historic landmarks and monuments!** While another sign way in the back screamed blatantly: **LET'S GO BACK TO THE DARK AGES AND END AFFIRMATIVE ACTION NOW!**

All this red-hot enthusiasm and roaring, overzealous support energized the young man to no end, making him smile ear-to-ear. He had found his true calling, his mission, right in this very moment on this stage, his confidence and self-esteem boosted by the loud chants and cheers.

The haircut the young man wore was clean and neat with a military sheen to it. It was a style that was wildly popular among white nationalists. Some would categorize this peculiar haircut as hipster while others would define it as Nazi-like.

White nationalists sported this haircut, coined as the "Fashy Haircut", at rallies and political conferences. This was the new look of the modern-day Nazi, the new 'do combined with a three-piece Brooks Brothers suit. Some even referred to the cut as the "Hitler Youth", because of its resemblance to the popular style worn during Germany's Third Reich.

The young man maintained his broad grin as he stepped up to a microphone on the stage and said, "Thank you! Thank you for coming today, folks. Your attendance means the world to us. Your participation in each and every event helps build and solidify the movement and makes it stronger and stronger and more united. Kudos to those of you who came today despite having to endure those nasty and dirty stares from people in your life that are *not* sympathetic towards this movement, of having to deal with outright hostility from those agents that are trying to sabotage and destroy this very cause. Shame on them! Pity those misunderstood and confused souls!"

The crowd roared back with cheers and applause.

The man paused for a moment, basking in the energy and support he was receiving, and making eye contact with as many people from the audience as he possibly could. *Super important. Need to continuously build the movement, to recruit and convert as many followers as possible. Build and spread the word, do continuous outreach, and keep the flames of momentum going. Strength in numbers.*

The man proudly gazed ahead at a giant banner that was tied up to a fence surrounding the enclosed space where he was permitted to speak today. That banner read: **Utopia Euro-West, Building and Securing White Culture for Today and Tomorrow**

He thought that line had a rather nice ring to it, if he didn't mind saying so himself. *Real nice.* It was his brainchild and moniker, after all. Let's not be modest about it.

The young man leaned closer to the microphone and added: "One of those agents that has been extremely critical and harsh on our movement is none other than one Claire Goldman."

That name alone elicited a number of vehement boos and hisses from the crowd.

"Due to the incredibly damaging *exposé* in a book she wrote," he continued. "Which includes erroneous and embellished profiles of our organization as well as others in the movement, she has managed to perpetuate and circulate lies about the cause."

More boos erupted from the audience.

The man looked at his fellow audience members and continued on with his fiery tirade: "In the book, as well as on numerous radio interviews, she has even gone as far as publicly vowing to putting an end to our organization and others like it and smearing more mud and lies about the cause in the process."

"Down with the witch!" a man shouted, and others immediately joined him on the chant.

A woman in the crowd interjected: "Should we try to educate her and set her straight?"

"Nooooooooo!" the audience rumbled back. *"Down with the witch!"* they kept chanting.

The young man standing on the stage smiled and nodded encouragingly at the crowd. This was just the beginning of many great things to come…oh, yes siree, this was just the beginning for sure. He had created a monster indeed and it would snowball for certain.

* * *

She experienced a second wind on the jog back to her apartment, feeling those endorphins kick in, that natural runner's high. Breathing in and out, in and out, in and out. She felt indestructible and immortal right now, as if she could tackle anything or anyone. God, she loved this feeling and wished it could last forever. That, and being able to take in the scenic beauty of Lake Merritt every day. She was incredibly thankful for that. She was deeply grateful for a lot of things in her life: her health, her family and friends, her amazing apartment with the awesome panoramic views of the lake, her career and all the achievements she had accomplished in the field of women's studies and feminist activism.

After wiping the beads of perspiration from her forehead and face with the sleeve of her shirt Claire crossed the street to the steps of the Cleveland Cascade, right next to her apartment complex, and ascended the stairs at a brisk, steady pace. When she reached the very top of the steps she spun around and jogged back down. When she arrived back at the bottom landing on Lakeshore

Avenue less than a minute later, she turned around and climbed her way back up, completing six sets of this.

After catching her breath and stretching a little she headed back to her apartment, settling back into reality again and the daily grind and routine of her life. Honestly, she wouldn't trade it for anything in the world. Claire suddenly thought of the second letter she received as she climbed the stairs to her floor. The thought of it rattled and shook her back to reality, to her inner core, and made her feel vulnerable and fragile once more. She no longer felt indestructible and immortal and didn't feel like she could tackle anything anymore.

I'd better call Albert, she thought, as she walked down the hallway to her apartment's door. *And check and see if he's heard back from the lab about the letters.*

When Claire inserted her key into the door's keyhole to turn the deadbolt lock, she noticed that it did not turn as she expected it to, for it was already unlocked.

She frowned immediately. *"What?"* she asked in disbelief, surprised and a little shocked, for she definitely remembered locking the door when she exited her unit earlier. She did not imagine or hallucinate it. She was absolutely certain she had locked the door because she recalled she had checked and shook it a couples of times to make sure it was indeed locked. Yes, she remembered that part vividly. Something did not feel right here and she hesitated for a moment, trying to decide what the best course of action should be. She was getting bad vibes from this. Her gut told her to just leave right now, not go in at all, and go straight to Albert's house instead. But then a part of her wanted to make sure her apartment was okay and that it had not been burglarized. This was Oakland, after all, and crime occurred here as it did in any other city. Unfortunately, it just so happened Oakland always got a bad reputation in the news.

Or another option was to go to her neighbor's apartment down the hall, ask her if she saw or heard anything unusual, and ask her to accompany her to her unit. That was a good idea because situations like this were usually safer in pairs or groups. So Claire decided to do just that, walking down the corridor until she reached the door at the very end, and knocked on it.

She waited a moment before knocking again, trying to remain calm and rational. Still no answer and no sound from behind the door, either. Another idea came to her: she could call the police but Lord knew how long it would take for them to get here considering all the urgent crimes they had to prioritize. Her matter would probably wind up at the bottom of the ladder in all likelihood.

She quietly headed back to her door and her hand slowly reached out towards the doorknob and took it gently. After hesitating once more, trying to remain calm, her hand slowly turned the knob and carefully pushed the door open. She peered inside her apartment but did not see anything out of the ordinary from the crack in the doorway. She pushed the door open further, taking the first step into the unit, moving like she was walking on eggshells. She got a better view of her living room at this point and so far nothing appeared to be out of place or stolen, at least from the naked eye.

Claire kept moving, taking cautious steps forward, like she was looking out for landmines on the floor. Then two things struck her immediately when she was about five yards into the apartment, allowing the door to close quietly. First, she noticed that the living room window was open and she knew she did not open it. Secondly, the further and further she probed into the unit the more she noticed a foul and pungent odor inside and it seemed to be emanating from somewhere in the back. She winced and wrinkled her nose at the stench. Funny, because she didn't recall leaving any spoiled food or garbage out. Her stomach muscles had tensed and she was completely on guard as she tip toed around, half expecting some crazed home invaders in ski masks to come charging out of the bedroom with guns waving but nothing of the sort occurred. *Still, I'm crazy as shit to be doing this alone!* she mused. *You've got guts, woman!*

She slowly made her way past the bend to the kitchen and that's when her eyes widened and her jaw dropped open to issue out a bloodcurdling scream that shattered the eerie silence. For lying on the kitchen table was the bloody and dismembered remains of a large cat, and hanging from a length of twine from the ceiling light and fan was the animal's severed head. Scrawled in what appeared to be blood on the white wall near the kitchen table were the words: **Die, you kike bitch! Die, pig!** And below that were some weird symbols and a message, also written in blood, which appeared to be in Latin or some other ancient language.

CHAPTER SIX

Albert looked at the hostile and nasty words that were written on the wall. Then he studied the weird symbols and the message.

Claire, standing close to him, practically hip to hip as though they were Siamese twins, leaned into his left ear and asked softly: "What does it mean?" Close enough that he felt her warm breath on his ear. Her actions and behavior were, he deduced, a result of the fear and trauma she was still experiencing from the incident. Which was completely understandable, of course. Something horrible like that would unnerve and rattle anybody. And he never minded it one bit when she was touching him, skin to skin or otherwise.

"Satan worshippers," he replied.

She furrowed her brow. *"Huh?"*

He pointed at the ancient language. "That's Latin for, 'Die, you kike bitch! Die, pig!' And then along with that is a reference to the end of days, the apocalypse, and that you will go to purgatory."

She stared at the message. "Oh, jeez! How original! Nothing but a bunch of pathetic, primitive losers." Then she turned away, shaking her head with wretched sadness. "And the cat! Poor thing. Why'd they have to slaughter the cat like that? It didn't do anything wrong. It was harmless in all this."

"Sacrifice of animals is very common in Satanism," he replied grimly.

A moment later, there was a knock on her apartment door and she walked over to open it. Standing in the doorway were two police officers.

One of them, a tall black man with a shaved and gleaming head that resembled a billiard ball, nodded at her pleasantly. "Good evening, ma'am."

"Please, come in," Claire said.

The police officers came inside the unit where she showed them the dead cat and the messages, before proceeding further about what had actually happened upon her return from her run.

After the tall cop took down her statement he went ahead and took some photographs of the cat and of the blood on the wall.

Albert watched the officer, quickly finding Claire's soft and warm hand and grabbing it, squeezing it with meaning and urgency. "From this point on you'll be staying with me at my house. You'll be safer there."

She squeezed his hand back in return. "Wow, it's gonna be a full house with you, me, and those exchange students."

"That it will be."

***

September 1995, Columbia University, New York City

"Hey, whatcha reading, brainy girl?" Albert asked, approaching the study table.

Claire, her face buried in her textbook, which was full of highlighted paragraphs and sentences, finally shook herself out of her state of complete and extreme focus and concentration and looked up at him. She had been so immersed in the book that she hadn't seen or heard him coming at all. So focused that she had been totally oblivious of her surroundings, in fact, with her laptop, notebook, pens, pencils, eraser, folders, backpack, and other textbooks (lots of them) scattered all over the cubicle table in the Lawrence Wein reference room in the Butler Library, literally infringing on the personal space of the fellow student she shared the table with.

Her eyes widened and her jaw dropped open when she finally saw and realized just how territorial, ignorant, and rude she had been, snatching and dragging her stuff back to her side of the table like she was a child caught in the act and had been reprimanded and had to gather all her toys and go back to her room. Trying to correct the problem swiftly. She turned to the student sitting next to her, apologizing profusely.

"I'm *so* sorry for encroaching on your space!" Claire said softly, trying to keep her voice down in the sacred and sanctified silence of the library. "My bad!"

The student, who appeared to be an international exchange student from Africa, simply smiled it off, as if she had done absolutely nothing wrong, dismissing the act all together like it had never happened or like he had not even noticed it.

"No problem," the student said.

She turned back to Albert, sighing. "I've been up to my eyeballs, literally, with papers, papers, *reading, reading*, and more *reading*," she whispered. "Be a dear and throw me a life-jacket, would ya, and save me from drowning in all this paper."

Albert squatted down next to her so she didn't have to raise her voice. He looked at the mountainous pile of books in front of her. "Looks like you *clearly* need a break. Why don't we go grab some coffee or go for a walk? Getting some fresh air will do you wonders, believe me. Give your eyes some much needed rest."

Claire frowned miserably. "Don't tempt me now!" She shifted her gaze back to the thick textbook before her and to all those daunting chapters she had to cover before that crucial midterm, before turning to look at her laptop. Her brow furrowed as she looked at the screen, at the paper she was writing for another class. Another fire she had to extinguish before day's end. And the teacher for that class was as anal and as strict as they came so she knew she had to be on her 'A' game for that particular paper. *Oh, brother! Just keep breathing calmly and roll with the punches, girl*, she thought. *You got this.* "Oh, I've got so much to do," she added, staring at the screen and tapping some keys on the keyboard. "And the kicker is that all of it is due at pretty much the same time. Isn't that lovely?" Albert looked at her with sad, lovey-dovey eyes. "Oh, poor Claire!" he whispered. "Ahh, the typical, thankless life of a starving Columbia University student. I sympathize with you completely." He made a sweeping arc gesture with his arm at the length of the reference room. "I mean, hey, me and all these other students in here are in the same boat as you, okay? You're not alone."

Despite his reassurance, which she totally appreciated and needed, she kept frowning. After she finished typing several more sentences on the laptop, she paused and pursed her lips for a moment, debating...debating...pondering, before finally saving her work and shutting her laptop, and closing her myriad collection of books, scattered all about her like insects, and miraculously being able to stuff everything back into that backpack of hers.

She looked up at him and said, "Okay, buster, let's go. But I can't stay out for too long, okay? Just a short break and then I gotta hit the books again."

But as it later turned out, Claire never did return to the library to study, after all. Nor did she go back to her apartment right away to continue studying, for that matter. Instead, truth be told, she found herself hanging out with Albert longer than she expected to and longer than she should have (thoughts of her homework persistently hung over her head like dark and ominous rain clouds), mostly because she really enjoyed his company immensely. It lifted her spirits and she laughed more than she could remember in a long, long time, laughed so much, in fact, that her belly ached. Claire, still fretting and freaking out about those homework assignments, decided to just go with the flow and enjoy the present moment. Enjoyed the bliss and laughter. *Is this what it's like to be in love?* she wondered.

First, they did grab a cup of joe at a local café off campus and then strolled down the street. And suddenly, a thought occurred to her, as it often did, sometimes during the most unexpected and awkward moments, as they were walking and she glanced at her watch. During the whole time he had his arm around her shoulders but she didn't mind. He even massaged those stiff and sore shoulders of hers, stiff from all that unhealthy sitting when she was studying, hunched and bent over her laptop, kneading out the knots and aches with his strong and firm hands. Those wonderful, magical hands of his.

"*Mmmmmmmmm*, whatever you're doing, don't stop!" Claire purred, closing her eyes and smiling.

He grinned. "Glad that you appreciate my handiwork."

"Say, we can kill two birds with one stone, maybe even three, so to speak," she began. "You said you like board games, open mics, and beer, right?"

"Uh-huh." His magic hands kept doing their thing on her shoulders and back, bless his heart.

"There's a cool, little bar over in the Village that I think you'll enjoy," Claire said. "And it's right near this new vegetarian Indian restaurant I've been dying to try. You game?"

"I saw you eat meat the other day!" It sounded more like an accusation, and a slightly sarcastic one at that, coming from him rather than a statement of fact. He was totally guilt tripping her and ribbing her, of course.

She blushed a little. "I know, I know. Well, it's something I've been wanting to explore, is all. I'm leaning towards healthier eating nowadays."

"Sure, let's do it."

"Awesome!" she replied, leading the way to the cool and drafty confines of the nearby 116th Street subway station where they caught a train to the Village. The station and the tunnels were a very welcome relief and escape from the sticky humidity above ground. She could've done without the crowded train, though. Didn't care for it at all and wished all the sweaty and warm bodies surrounding her would just vanish into the ether. All packed in there tightly like sardines. Some dude's smelly armpit, complete with his perspiration bleeding through onto the damp upper sleeve of his shirt in the shape of a crescent, was arched right over her head. *Talk about major yuck factor!* But that was New York City for you. One of the things about living in the big, bad city. All the people, all the people. The masses.

Fortunately, the ride down to the Village was smooth and relatively short. And before she knew it, she and Albert were off the subway car, breathing fresh air again, and climbing up the stairs to the street level. Once she got her bearings straight she led the way down to the bar where a sign above the front entrance read: **Four Leaf Clover**.

While Claire ordered the drinks at the bar, with Albert initially creating a minor scene trying to prove he was a true and stellar gentleman (and that chivalry still existed in this day and age), of which she had no single doubt of, by wanting to pay for the beverages. In fact, he was quite insistent about it, even to the point of getting into her face, but in the end he capitulated and allowed her to pay.

She smiled at him. "My treat, buddy."

He managed to snag them a private corner table where they huddled close together like a meeting of the minds, all nice and cozy, to play a round of a fantasy strategy board game, one of a plethora the bar had in their game collection. She rolled the dice first, shaking it firmly in her hand, and let it land on the board.

Lucky six.

Claire took a sip of her beer before moving her figure, which happened to be a Viking king sort of character with a two-horned helmet to boot, down the necessary number of spaces to the embankment of a river.

"I don't mean to break your concentration," Albert started, raising his voice a little amid the raucous and boisterous atmosphere of the bar, jukebox blaring and all. "But just curious, why'd you pick this particular game?"

She leaned forward a little more so he could hear her response. "Hey, you're talking to a nerdy girl who grew up playing lots of Dungeons and Dragons and video games. I was even a member of my high school's D&D club."

"Did you guys have club badges and membership cards?"

She nodded enthusiastically, getting her geek on. "We sure did."

"Talk about hard core."

She lifted her glass and drank some more beer. "That we were. Sometimes we even dressed up in costumes like the characters when we played."

"I'd love to see pictures of that, if you have any." He moved his figure forward a few paces, which eventually got him into a real hairy situation, and lost his opportunity to advance further for the time being.

Claire clasped her hands together and eagerly retrieved the dice and rolled them. *C'mon, lucky number now!* She got a four and moved her figure.

He smiled mischievously. "Hey, just a thought, but if I win this game will you let me come over to your apartment?"

She broke her fixed gaze on the board, raised her head up, and looked at him, considering his question for a moment. "Oh, the rain check!"

"And don't forget the kosher meal," he reminded her.

She looked at him once more before rolling the dice and moving the figure again. "It slipped my mind. Sorry!" Thought about it some more. "Well, yeah, that sounds like a fair deal to me. But that's *if* you win." She smirked at him.

They took in all the ambiance and charm of the little bar in the Village, for as well as playing the board game, which Albert *did* win, by the way, the two also indulged themselves in a simple game of darts, and checked out the poets, rappers, and spoken word artists at the open mic show in the small lounge area. Albert bought them another round of beers.

Claire clinked her glass against his. "Good job!" she said. "Kudos for kicking my ass!"

He winked at her, taking a sip of his beer. "Pretty good for a first-time player of the game, huh?"

"Damn straight!" she replied, raising her glass to salute him like he had just won the Super Bowl and was just bestowed the prestigious honor of MVP. But truthfully, she had to admit the alcohol had gotten to her and bit her in the ass, making her feel giddy and silly. A nice buzz, though, like she was floating through space or something.

"This calls for a special celebration!" she added, thinking that the booze was partially speaking through her now and making her appear a little goofy. The other half was totally serious and sincere about how she really felt. "To celebrate your victorious and glorious win, Royal Prince Albert, you are formally and cordially invited to the epic grand palace, *errr* castle, of Queen Claire, Your Royal Majesty." She beamed ear-to-ear like she was standing before her loyal and faithful followers and minions of the court. "Where you will wine, dine, and swoon to an epic five-course Jewish family style meal." Claire made a face, a cross between a cringe and a wince (maybe that was the beer's fault as well), like she had just committed a major faux pas. Trying to stay in character and keep the momentum flowing, she quickly interjected, "*Correction*: will wine, dine, and swoon to your heart's content and have major fun! In fact, you *will* have fun, *guaranteed*."

Albert smiled at her like he had just won the lottery. "I accept your invitation wholeheartedly," he replied.

She peered at him mischievously through the top half of her glass like she was playing an innocent, little game of hide-and-seek with him. "Invitation confirmed, Royal Prince Albert. Shall I send my driver and carriage to pick you up?"

"Please do. That would be most appreciated, Queen Claire."

CHAPTER SEVEN

Robert leaned closer to his computer's keyboard and quickly pecked out a response to the latest comment on the forum's message board. The name of the forum was at the top of the screen, written in retro-style font in the form of shiny gold letters made to appear like sacred and holy bars of gold: **Utopia Euro-West**.

The question he had posed on today's thread was, "What kind of weapon do you plan on bringing to the Unite Whites Rally?"

And a horde of new notifications and messages poured in. The floodgates had been released and there was no holding back now. It was awesome to see this kind of enthusiastic reaction and feedback, to know that there were so many like-minded followers out there that adored and loved his show and shared his opinions. It excited him to no end to know that there were others who were as hardcore about the cause as he was, and to know that he was not the only one in this world that had these passionate feelings for the cause and that he was not the only one that held this viewpoint. And thank God for this amazing technology, this World Wide Web and dark web, for smart phones, for tablets, for the web cam, and apps and apps galore that kept them all connected and cohesive and informed them about all the latest happenings in their community.

Robert immediately 'liked' **Giant Blonde Viking's** comment: "*Sword!* The streets will be awash with blood! Cleanse out all that antifa bacteria!"

Another user named **Luftwaffe** punched in the following feedback: "Sledgehammer!"

Robert clicked the 'like' button next to that comment.

Yet another user, whose avatar username read, **Heinrich Himmler Junior**, fired in a comment that said: "Machete!"

That earned him a 'like' by Robert as well, who nodded encouragingly at that kind of fervor and zest and that kind of reply. He leaned back in his office chair, gently patting the top of the soft blonde surface of the "Fashy Haircut" he sported, watching with an almost hypnotized kind of awe and fascination as the plethora of responses continued to populate the screen in a mad frenzy exactly the way he had hoped for. *Wow, this is fucking incredible!* he thought. *Bring it on!*

Leaning forward, he typed out another response. Then he opened up another tab on the screen and jumped over to the website for his online talk radio show, signing in as **Moderator**. He looked at the clock. *Almost show time, boys and girls.* Robert smiled, clasping his hands together like an expectant father at his pregnant wife's bedside.

Robert moved the cursor over to a button on the computer screen and clicked on it. "Hey, good evening, boys and girls, welcome to another edition of Utopia Euro-West!" he said into the microphone (followed by a short audio sample of composer Richard Wagner's "Ride of the Valkyries," which was then followed by a brief and generic clip of enthusiastic cheering and applause), with more mustard and zeal than he actually intended to, which was all good. Nothing bad about that. In his book nothing was worse than sounding like a complete and utter bore. And a dull and obtuse bore at that. Yawn! He was here to entertain, inform, and educate, not put the masses to sleep for crying out loud! Just now, he sounded a bit like a seasoned radio drama actor or a podcast performer. That was the effect he was aiming for. A little bit of Orson Welles and a little dose of Richard Spencer mixed in.

"Okay, tonight, boys and girls, we don't have a set agenda or theme per se," Robert continued. "Tonight we're going to leave the forum wide open for you to discuss and tackle whatever's on your mind. What pressing topics are you itching to talk about? What would you like to hurl off your chest that is a major concern for you? We here at Utopia Euro-West *want* to know about it. Our listeners *want* to know about it. We want to let you know that *you* are *not* alone out there, that you have fellow brothers and sisters, friends, and like-minded folks who are in the same boat as you and want to hear what you have to say regarding the advancement of the white race, the white culture, and how best to preserve and protect it from evil entities that wish to destroy and eradicate it. We always hear about how minorities are always trying to safeguard and treasure social service programs beneficial to them, historical landmarks, statues, buildings, and sites and such. Well, what about our history and our historic landmarks and statues?

Who's going to help protect us?" He let a profound pause sink in. Letting that gravity make itself known among the masses and allowed it to digest in the brains of his listeners. "Looks like no one's going to assist us, doesn't it? Just take a look at what happened in Charlottesville and you'll understand. Those animals pillaged and plundered our historic monuments, remember? Yes, they did indeed and not a single day passes by that we do *not* forget, do we?"

Suddenly, the bar graphs and lines on his computer screen lit up like wildfire as calls began queuing up like mad. As always, Robert raised his eyebrows, impressed by the immediate, out-of-the-gate response. "Okay, let's go to caller number one, Daniel from Salem, Oregon. What's your two-cents for tonight, Daniel? We're dying to know."

"First and foremost on my mind tonight, Robert, is the pressing matter of that troublesome and annoying feminist scholar, writer, and activist, Claire Goldman. You know, the one that wrote that scathing book about our movement where she's literally attacking our very ideals, goals, and all the values we stand for, which are legally protected under the Constitution, by the way. We have a right to those very ideas, in case she conveniently forgot. She's trying to shut us down single-handedly, a one-woman entity trying to smother out our voices and concerns, our dreams and aspirations to build a better world and future for our culture and for our children."

Robert leaned closer to the microphone. "That's right, Daniel," he confirmed.

"People like her make my stomach turn and make me wanna puke," Daniel muttered with disgust.

"Yeah, well, you're not alone in your opinion, my friend. A lot of us, a vast majority, in fact, share your viewpoint concerning Miss Goldman."

"So what are we gonna *do* about it?" Daniel asked, almost challenging him to take some sort of corrective action to deal with the problem at hand. Throwing it on him now to fix it. To resolve it once and for all it seemed.

Robert paused for a moment before saying cryptically, "Rest assured, steps are being taken to remedy the issue."

* * *

Claire's belongings, all boxed, packaged, and bundled together, sat in the foyer and living room of Albert's house, waiting to be attended to and sorted. What a strange and timely coincidence, for not that many days ago, less than two weeks, in fact, Pei and Lee's personal possessions rested in roughly the same area after they had arrived on these foreign shores and set foot inside this very same home. At first, Albert was rather nervous and apprehensive about having new guests at his house, the exchange students in particular (which was weird because he had hosted exchange students before in the past and didn't know why these feelings suddenly sprang up), but *now* those feelings of foreboding had disappeared and he had gotten used to the concept and had actually experienced a change of heart regarding the matter rather quickly. Which was also kind of strange, too.

To say that he had adapted or acclimated to the situation might be another good way to describe it. Change was a good and positive thing in his book. Sometimes it could be negative. One thing was certain: he definitely had no problems about Claire moving in with him, whether it was on a permanent basis or temporary. Absolutely none whatsoever. She was his ex-wife, after all, someone he knew, had known, and someone he could trust. An old flame that he did not mind having as a new flame in his life again. Time would tell about that. He didn't quite know how to broach that topic with Claire just yet. His gut told him she'd be open and receptive to it, generally speaking, and could imagine her welcoming and embracing it. But then again, it had been a long time since they had been together romantically, let alone living with one another, and they had both changed and aged as people over time, so maybe she would *not* even want to entertain the idea. Maybe deep down inside in her inner core (the part of her that she did not reveal to him), marriage and divorce had left a sour taste in her mouth and tainted her impression and vision of him, and maybe having been married together in the past was more than enough for her and she would not want to get involved with him again. Maybe getting back together again was the last thing on her mind. She definitely had a lot on her plate now with these death threats. And besides, they weren't twentysomething college students anymore who thought they were invincible and indestructible. The world around them had changed and evolved dramatically. So who knew? *Time will tell*, he kept telling himself. *Time will tell.*

He returned to the here and now, standing in the living room and looking at her belongings, studying her familiar handwriting on the boxes (in black marker pen to label what the contents were), with the rather loopy *Ss* and elongated *Ts*. He even recognized an old suitcase of hers from their old college days, a little battered and dusty but still usable from the looks of it. He stepped over to it and slowly ran his fingers along the surface of that suitcase, sparking a little trip down nostalgia lane to her sunny apartment that faced the west, near the Columbia University campus. Closing his eyes for a moment, he could still feel the sunny warmth of that unit, could feel those rays of light on his face, by mere memory and recall alone and could still smell the mouthwatering aroma of freshly baked bread wafting in from the kitchen. One of Claire's culinary concoctions.

Suddenly, the short foray of his time travel daydream, and just when it was getting good, too, was abruptly shattered when Claire opened the front door of his house and came in with a couple of bags in her hands. More stuff. Her short dark brown hair, peppered with occasional strands of white, was fashioned in the style of a 1980s mullet, complete with bangs and all. She resembled one of his favorite childhood actresses, Geneviève Bujold.

"Well, that's all of it," she said, putting the bags down on the coffee table, standing there in a smooth and silky black sleeveless blouse, a slightly modish, Swinging London-type black skirt, and knee-length black leather boots. Looking as hot and gorgeous as ever. Appearing as beautiful and striking as the first day he ever laid eyes on her. She frowned and took a deep breath. "I'm being driven out of my own home, made to feel frightened and intimidated by these people...and in the process I'm imposing on you and your time." She shook her head, looking at the floor. "I'm so sorry...I shouldn't let them get to me like this. Don't you see? I'm doing exactly what they want by showing them my fear and scurrying out of my place like a coward."

Albert walked over to her and gently put his arm around her shoulders. She leaned closer to him, putting her head on his shoulder.

"I should be fighting back," she added, with venom in her voice. "Not fleeing from my own home like this."

He turned his head slightly and kissed the top of her head. "I think that would be an unwise move. You clearly see how disturbed and sick these people are by the work they left you. Why provoke them and get yourself in harm's way? Best to let the police handle it now."

She didn't respond right away and with the silence that ensued he could sense her listening to and digesting his words, trying to listen to the voice of reason, logic, and rationale, like she usually did when she was quiet and analytical like this. "The cops offered to have a patrol car swing by every day to watch my apartment," she said. "That was nice of them. But not to send an officer or officers and monitor me around the clock."

"They don't have the manpower for that," he explained. "I mean, it's Oakland. Think about all the high priority crimes they have to deal with."

Claire turned and looked up at him with a hurt look on her face that proclaimed, 'Hey, I'm someone!'. "Hey, I'm sort of a celeb, a known writer, figure, and activist in the feminist rights movement. I mean, there's even a Wikipedia page about me. Plus, I have a considerable amount of followers on Facebook and Twitter. You'd think that would account for something in this day and age." She paused. "But maybe the police aren't big on us feminists, huh? We're still viewed as troublemakers and rebels of the counterculture scene, aren't we?"

He kissed the top of her head again. "Not to me you're not. The police have their own agenda." He kissed her once more. "Don't worry, I'll protect you, babe."

She smiled at him. "Thanks. But remember, I'm a strong, independent woman and can take care of myself as well, you know. You're not put off or offended by that, are you? I should think not for I've known you for this long to know all your little quirks, nuances, and mannerisms."

"That's right. If there's anyone that can see right through me, see me inside out, or look into my soul it would be you." He leaned closer to her and kissed her, on the lips this time.

It appeared to him that Claire liked what she tasted because she licked her lips with sultry satisfaction and based on that eager, red-flushed glow on her cheeks and face, her eyes shimmering with rekindled passion. Her forehead nice and warm against his, pressed so tight against his brow that he could feel her healthy pulse. It seemed like she really dug it, in fact, for she instinctively reached over and kissed him with more fervor and passion this time, even going so far as sticking her tongue into his mouth and probing and exploring. It had been a while since they engaged in foreplay like this. A real long time, longer than he could remember.

To him, this was fun and this was what he wanted right now. She turned her head and looked around them, showing that she was making sure that no one was watching them, appearing like a naughty teenage girl up to no good. That look also reminded him of that free-spirited, twentysomething college student in New York City that he fell in love with so many years ago. So long ago that it seemed like another lifetime now.

Claire whispered to him, "Are we alone?"

"Yes. Pei and Lee are on campus, I believe."

"So we've got the whole house to ourselves, huh?" she purred into his ear.

"Yep," he whispered back into her ear.

After he said that she grabbed his belt, her hands clumsy and klutzy at first, fumbling around for a second or two before finally managing to unhook it successfully, before she unzipped his fly and pulled his pants and underwear off clean.

And voila! There it was...Claire just stood there for a moment and stared at his fully erect manhood, mesmerized by it like she had never seen a man's genitals before. Then she grabbed it and began stroking it fast while Albert quickly began unbuttoning her blouse, his fingers moving with a smooth, confident, and brisk dexterity.

* * *

"Oh God, that was fucking amazing!" Albert said, as he lay in bed staring up at the ceiling. He sighed in exhaustion. "I don't think I can take this anymore."

Claire, laying there beside him, naked and sweaty, laughed. "Your old, creaky bones and my old, creaky bones can't take it anymore." Her hand submerged itself under the rumpled and disheveled blanket like a submarine's periscope, found his penis again, and continued fondling it.

He shook his head, arching his eyebrows in an expression of awe. "Man, your libido hasn't changed since college! Are you experiencing a second wind of your twenties or something? You're like the Energizer bunny!"

She laughed again. "Must be all that healthy living I'm engaged in. All those endorphins." She stared up at the ceiling, too, still running on and feeling that natural high of sex, feeling a mixture of giddiness and being dazed, but in a good way. She pursed her lips philosophically, pausing to think for a moment. "Remember when back in the day we used to smoke a joint after we had sex and would talk for a bit in bed?"

Albert nodded. "That gave the experience a nice, final touch, in a way." He smiled in recollection. "I always enjoyed our conversations about everything under the sun. I felt like I could talk to you about anything that was on my mind and loved that feeling of trusting you and not having to censor or edit myself."

She grinned, turning to him and shooting him a lovestruck look, like they were falling in love all over again even though they had known each other like forever. "*Awww*, you're so sweet, Albert! Thank you. I felt that, too…I think we were, and still are, kindred spirits."

"You mean like we were made for each other or were destined to meet?"

"Uh-huh."

He was silent for just a moment but that stillness was definitely palpable. "Then why did we break up? Why the divorce?" She noticed the sadness, the disappointment, in the tone of his voice. It made her gloomy as well.

Surprisingly, she found her response to his question was calm, measured, and well thought out. And hopefully not clichéd. "I think we went too fast too soon and burned ourselves out. Even though we clicked really well with one another, we rushed things and didn't see the consequences coming. And when you're young like that, like we were, that's a volatile and dangerous mix. There's an old saying that goes, when you're having too much of a good thing no matter how great it is, indulging in too much of it will hurt you in the end."

"Truth!" he said. "You hit the nail right on the head."

"Damn straight!" She nodded for emphasis. "I think we learned from our mistakes." At least she hoped that they did. She, in her heart's heart, felt that she certainly did. Claire noticed that he was visibly silent for a moment after that. "What are you thinking about?" she asked curiously.

Albert cleared his throat and she knew he was having a difficult time bringing whatever was on his mind out into the light. She definitely sensed that. Like the words were stuck in his throat or something.

"And we were and have always been honest with each another," she reminded him, as if he needed to be prompted for that. Now, surely, he will open up to her.

He propped himself up one elbow, looking at her admiringly. "Well, this is definitely timely because I've rehearsed this scene in my head recently."

She turned and lay on her side, giving him her full and undivided attention now.

"Well, what I wanted to talk to you about was us getting back together again," he started quietly. "I didn't know if you're receptive to that or not."

Claire smiled a little, touched by this. "You mean getting back together in a regular sense or getting married again?" Clarification was always important.

"I meant being a couple again. Being in a relationship."

She reached over and massaged his thigh. "I thought we already were, hon. We didn't quite say it in X amount of words but I thought it was mutually sensed and acknowledged between us, if you know what I mean."

He nodded. "It was but I just wanted to make sure, that's all." He smiled. "I just wanted to hear it officially from you."

She slowly crawled on top of him, still sweaty and sticky, allowing his erect penis to ease itself gently inside of her. Then she leaned down and kissed him passionately on the lips, her tongue probing into his mouth. "Well, now you have, babe."

Moments later, the bedsprings started creaking like mad again.

CHAPTER EIGHT

Albert took Claire's hand as they strolled down to the local café near his house. It was a few short blocks along the main drag, San Pablo Avenue. She was dressed nicely today, in his humble opinion (but he was biased, of course, because he thought she looked great all the time), in a black colored blouse with purple stripes across the front of it, a red leather skirt, and dark brown boots.

During the walk there, she squeezed his hand and said, "Hey, guess what? I heard back from the police about the letters and about that gruesome mess that was discovered in my apartment."

"What did they say?" he asked. He kind of had an idea but let her speak.

"Well, they didn't find any fingerprints on the two letters or *any* prints in my apartment, for that matter. Aside from my own, of course."

He frowned. "That's what I figured. We're dealing with pros here who were wise enough to wear gloves. Did the police say anything else?"

"That the letters were composed using standard word processing software," she added. "Standard font and all that and using regular copier paper."

"A much smarter method, than say, handwriting a letter," Albert remarked. "Less chance of it being traced back to the writer."

"How do you outwit these maniacs?"

He turned and looked at her. "By not giving in to their demands."

She nodded. "Does that include sticking it in their faces, too?"

He suppressed a grin. "Hmm, there goes your vindictive alter ego again. Remember what I said. Be careful with that."

They reached the café minutes later. After Albert exchanged brief pleasantries with the owner, who he knew but hardly ever saw anymore except for on rare occasions such as this, and introducing Claire to her, he ordered citrus green tea for the both of them (one of her favorites) and a Danish that they shared. They grabbed a small table in the quiet patio in the back with its calm, soothing water fountain and abundance of potted plants and flowers.

Claire glanced at her watch before sipping some of the hot tea.

"What time do you have to leave for your evening class?" he asked.

"Around four or four thirty."

"To beat that traffic, huh? Hey, tell you what, I'll drive you to the campus tonight. We can talk on the way there."

She dismissed that with a wave of her hand. "Oh, you don't have to do that! It's your night off after a long, hard day of teaching. Kick back and relax. I'll be back home before you know it. Plus, I have to make a pit stop at my apartment on the way back to get my phone charger and a few other things I forgot to bring with me."

He grabbed her hand. "Please don't go back there! I don't want you to. I'm getting negative vibes from that place now because of what happened."

"I'll just be in and out of there in a flash," she reassured him. "My phone's down to less than ten percent battery life! I need that charger."

"I'll buy you one and save you the trip," he offered, somewhat pleadingly. He knew he sounded totally desperate and bet that he looked it, too.

Claire chuckled, drinking more tea. "You're so silly! Don't waste your money...I'll be okay, really. I'll be really careful, I promise."

"You'd better be," he reminded her. "I just think you're walking into a trap of some sort. They have eyes on your apartment, not to mention access to it as well, and based on the hostile tone of those letters Lord knows what they have planned for you next. I'm here to make sure you remain safe."

She took a deep breath, her chin hovering over the cup of tea, as she brooded over something. Finally, she muttered to him, "Okay, okay, you can accompany me to the campus." But she said it rather begrudgingly like, 'I like you a lot but I really don't need a babysitter.'

Albert smiled gratefully. "Thank you, hon. You just made my day."

* * *

He drove her Mercedes convertible across the Bay Bridge into San Francisco, where traffic was surprisingly brisk and smooth in the late afternoon hours, which was completely the opposite of what she thought or expected it would be. Lucky for them. She kept looking out the passenger side window of the car for the duration of the journey across the bridge, gazing at all the little sailboats that dotted the surface of the water, appearing like toys floating in a bathtub. Her eyes then shifted to the beautiful and majestic skyline of the city itself, taking in the pointed tip of the Transamerica Pyramid building to the futuristic gleam and roundness of the Sales Force Tower. She looked at the people, resembling miniature model figures in a diorama, inside the various high-rise apartment and office buildings that made up the bulk of that skyline. She wondered what they were talking about, what important topics they were discussing at high-powered, executive meetings, and what kind of lives these folks led.

The sound of Albert's voice brought her out of her warm, fuzzy cocoon of daydreaming and back to the here and now.

"What are you thinking about?" he asked quietly.

"Oh, just lost in my own little world of make believe," she replied. "Nothing too exciting or glamorous, you know." *Trying to escape the stresses of the death threats by not thinking about it constantly.*

"Well, if it's coming from within you it surely must be exciting and fun. Tell me about it. Enlighten me a little."

She turned and saw his smile encouraging her to go on and elaborate, to entertain him.

Claire reciprocated a grin of her own, one that was rather coy. "Well, okay, if you insist."

"I do, my dear."

"That's fine" she said. "I was living vicariously through the lives of the people I see in those buildings." She nodded at the skyline and frowned. "But I don't think I'd like being behind all that glass at such a high level, especially in earthquake country. That's something I'll never quite get used to, being a New Yorker."

He nodded. "I hear ya. Nothing gets the heart pumping faster than tall, swaying buildings, lemme tell ya. And that's coming from a native Californian who's experienced several big quakes."

Claire looked out the window again. "Still, I love it here...there's something unique and magical about this place. For starters, I love the multicultural diversity of the Bay Area. That's something we have in abundance in New York as well, as you know. Secondly, the progressive liberalism and politics here is awesome. I wouldn't have it any other way. Being in a community with other like-minded folks is where I want to be now and being able to connect with those other people and exercise my right to organize and attend rallies, all for a good cause of shutting down the fascist right. And this is definitely a safe haven for doing that."

"Playing devil's advocate for a second," Albert said, hitting the left turn signal of the car before getting into the next lane over. They had arrived at the San Francisco end of the bridge and were coasting smoothly along highway 101 now. "Think about how those conservatives must feel the same way, of wanting to be able to voice their opinions and concerns just like you do. I don't agree with them one bit but I'm just showing the comparison, that's all."

"Duly noted, but you have to realize just how out of control, violent, and nasty the fascists have become," she explained. "Just watch the news and you'll see how they've taken this thing to a whole different level."

"Okay, we better stop talking about politics now before we tear each other's throats apart," he chuckled.

Knowing that was God's honest truth, for they had argued and debated like this before in the past, she simply nodded and buttoned her lips.

"On a totally different note," Albert remarked. "Your car runs pretty good considering its age." He raised his eyebrows. "Nice ride indeed."

"Thank you." She smiled modestly, appraising the interior surroundings of the Mercedes with an admiring eye. "I stay on top of all the maintenance and tune-ups, the majority of which I do myself." She maintained her smile. "Not trying to toot my own horn or anything but that's the honest truth. As a woman, I'm proud of that achievement."

He nodded.

The skies above had darkened by the time they arrived at San Francisco State University. Her watch read: five-thirty. Good timing. It gave her a nice, little cushion before her class started. After parking the car they went to her office in one of the newer, more modern buildings that had sprouted up on campus in the past couple of years. It was all shiny, gleaming, and reeked of state-of-the-art technology. And it still had that new building smell that would make some people giddy. But the place lacked that old-school soul and charm of the building that housed Albert's office, with its old, sticky linoleum tiled floors and antiquated doors, pipes, and water fountains. A dinosaur from way back when.

As they strode down a hallway on the ground floor, he looked up and was marveled by the lights. "Wow! Fancy."

"You ain't seen nothing yet," she said. "Wait till you come inside my office."

After disembarking the elevator on the third floor they strolled down yet another corridor with sparkling, polished floors and solid mahogany wood doors with sturdy steel doorknobs. When they reached a door that was almost at the end of the hallway she fished out a key from her purse and opened it. A card on a nameplate on the wall next to the door read: **Claire Goldman**. And listed the days and times she held office hours with students.

"Alexa, turn on the lights," she said as they stood in the darkness, and a second or two later the place was illuminated. The space was furnished with trendy, stylish furniture and sitting on her desk was an Apple desktop computer.

He raised his eyebrows, looking around the office. "Nice! Certainly puts my office to shame, thank you very much."

"And thank you, fellow tax and tuition payers," Claire added with a grin.

He sat down in one of the chairs in front of her desk, running his hands admiringly across the texture and craftsmanship of the upholstery. "So I guess I'll just preoccupy and entertain myself while you're working tonight."

She put her purse and hand bag on her desk before stepping over to sit on the edge of the desk, inches in front of him, touching and grazing his cheek gently and then his mouth, running her finger sensually and teasingly across his lips.

"You can use my computer," she said softly. "If you're hungry for reading material, which I always am when I'm sitting around and waiting, there's a pretty good selection of feminist literature on that bookshelf." She nodded at a bookshelf against one of the walls. "The restrooms are down the hall and there's a water fountain and a couple of snack machines next to it. Actually, I *did* bring a copy of my new book for you to read, as you requested." She rummaged the book out of her hand bag and gave it to him.

"Won't it be weird if students and staff see me here?" he inquired. "Strange man in your office?"

"Aw, screw them!" she muttered with a wave of her hand. "You're an important and special guest of mine. It's none of their business anyway."

Albert pulled her gently into his lap, wrapping his arms around her protectively. "Sure I'm not cramping your style, Teach?"

Claire leaned closer to his face and kissed him, a quick peck, on the lips. "Not in a million years." She checked her watch again, frowning a little. "*Aww!* It's getting close to that dreaded time!

I'd better get ready." She kissed him again before rising and grabbing her things.

* * *

"In her book, Scarborough theorizes that the three main reasons that women still do *not* report a rape is because, number one, they fear retaliation," Claire said, writing the word down on the chalkboard. "Number two is shame and guilt." She wrote the words on the chalkboard. "The victim thinks it's her fault that she got assaulted. That she, as the media so lovingly and frequently use the term, *'asked for it,'*" Claire cringed and made a face, raising her hands up in the air to emphasize quotation marks. "Whether that's because of the provocative or suggestive way they are dressed, or inadequately clothed or their lack of dress in some cases, including the way in which they use makeup, perfume, the behavior they utilize to conduct themselves in public, etc."

A woman sitting in the first row of the classroom sighed and mumbled, "Oh, brother! Give me a break!"

Claire turned to look at the student sympathetically. "I know. Unfortunately, a recent poll that was conducted of folks from a broad spectrum of ages and all walks of life still thinks that rape victims are the ones to blame and question for the crime and still thinks that victims had a hand in fabricating and manufacturing incidents."

This comment elicited an irritated groan from the same student sitting in the first row. "Boy, I thought we were living in 2020, *not 1920*," the student remarked.

Claire nodded and returned to the chalkboard before she lost her train of thought and momentum. "*And* the third reason is what Scarborough labels, or refers to, as the 'Happily Ever After' syndrome, in which the victim believes that things will get better and improve after the incident and that somehow, magically, spiritually, otherworldly or otherwise, that the attacker will eventually get caught and justice will be served. That karma exists for criminals and what goes around comes around full circle." She wrote this down on the chalkboard as well.

"Like they are denying the crime even occurred?" another student asked, her brow furrowing and her eyes widening in surprise.

"Yes," Claire answered grimly. "It happens. Because rape is such a traumatic and violent act, PTSD is involved in a great majority of the cases." She stepped over to a small table in front of the chalkboard to consult her notes. "And that's it for tonight, folks." She smiled. "You've been a great class as usual. Your homework assignment for this week is to read chapters five through eight in the Scarborough book and to get started on chapters one to four in the Hamner textbook." She looked at her students. "Okay? Any questions?"

A man, one of the few males in the class, nonchalantly said, "That's a lot of reading."

Claire shrugged. "Hey, this is a graduate-level college course. It is what it is."

As people began filing out of the classroom, Mavis, who had requested that Claire accompany her to her car in the parking garage earlier slowly approached her as she gathered her materials at the table.

"Hi," Mavis said quietly.

Claire looked up at her with a grin. "Hey!" She paused for a second before adding, "Mavis, correct?"

The student nodded. "Good memory."

"Well, I make it a point to remember every student's name and face. So, what's on your mind, Mavis?"

Mavis, noticeably shy and nervous, continued speaking in the same quiet tone of voice. "I was wondering if you could walk me to my car again."

Claire looked at her with concern. "Has there been another incident?"

"No, but I just feel a whole lot safer when I'm with someone in that dark, spooky garage."

"I know what you mean," Claire replied. "Give me a second here." She put her things in her hand bag and then grabbed her purse. "Okay, let's go." They strode down the corridor towards the bank of elevators. "I need to stop by my office first. My husband—" Claire immediately bit her tongue and corrected herself. "*Uhh*, my boyfriend is waiting for me there," she said, feeling a need to explain herself for some reason even though she didn't need to, least of all to a fellow student she hardly even knew. Maybe it was TMI. Too much information. But Mavis seemed like a nice enough person who'd understand. She was just a little scared, that's all. Nothing wrong with that in light of the attack that occurred on campus. And how timely and topical, too, considering the rape course she taught tonight.

When they arrived at her office she opened the door to discover Albert comfortably sitting in her office chair, feet crossed and propped up on one corner of that desk, reading her book like he was at a vacation resort or something.

He looked at her, the expression on his face conveying, 'Is it time to go already?? Just when the getting was good and all the nice, juicy details were being revealed in the book.'

Claire smiled at him. "Did you behave yourself?"

"I was a perfect gentleman, my dear," he replied, placing a bookmark in the book before shutting it. "A couple of your students even swung by and I kindly told them that you were in session and to come back during your assigned office hour times." He looked at Mavis, grinning, and said, "Hi, I'm Albert." Extending his hand to her.

"Mavis," she replied in that same quiet tone of hers. She shook his hand. Claire caught what appeared to be the slightest bit of disappointment and perhaps something else…maybe…maybe disgust, fear, or dread on Mavis's face, conveyed by a small but noticeable frown that was etched on her features, upon seeing Albert. *Maybe she doesn't like men or had a bad experience with one*, Claire thought. Mavis was, after all, a women's studies major, was probably a feminist like Claire, but then again, maybe she wasn't. *Don't generalize or judge people now.* But not everybody from those camps hated men. That was a terrible stereotype that had been perpetuated for far too long.

"We're just going to escort Mavis to her car," Claire explained, adding a little blurb about the assault that had happened on campus.

Albert frowned. "I understand. No problem at all."

The trio left the office and took the elevator back down to the ground level. Clusters of students were gathered around in the lobby area, talking or gossiping about this or that among themselves. Some lowered the tone of their voices to whispers when they saw Claire approaching. *Ahh, the student life*, Claire mused. *Been there and done that with Albert all those many years ago. Seems like another life now. Do I miss it? Ehhhh, yes and no. Would I want to jump in a time machine and revisit those old college days? Yes and no. College was tough and occasionally brutal and hellish! But, yes, definitely to all the times I had spent with Albert. Hands down on that one.* She figured the students were speaking in hushed tones now because of her and all the controversy her new book had stirred up. Not everybody at the university was happy and in agreement about the book, as liberal and progressive as San Francisco touted itself to be.

The three made it out of the hi-tech building and into the cool and breezy nighttime darkness, trekking down a paved path that snaked across the campus and led them down to the old parking structure that had seen much better days. Claire didn't blame Mavis one bit. This place was creepy as hell, especially at night. Good thing Mavis had asked for company. Strength in numbers, as the old saying went.

When they reached Mavis's vehicle on the second level of the garage Claire started getting a feeling...a strange feeling all of a sudden...call it female intuition or gut instinct, she felt it and it was telling her to get herself and Albert out of there immediately. *Run!* it told her.

The next thing she knew she heard tires screeching at break neck speed, the sound echoing throughout the parking garage, and saw something dark and monolithic rushing towards them like a high-speed missile. When she turned her head for a better look all she caught a glimpse of was a huge black car with its headlights off.

She shoved Albert and Mavis forward, out of harm's way, as the vehicle zoomed past them onto the spot where they would've been lying and left for dead had they not moved.

When she turned her head to look at the car again it was already long gone, swallowed up by the darkness of the parking structure, and leaving nothing behind except for the smell of burnt rubber and curls of smoke rising from the concrete floor.

Claire immediately returned her attention to her companions. "Are you two okay?"

"Yes," Albert replied.

Mavis nodded, staring ahead into space in a daze. "Wow, we could've been killed!" she said quietly.

"Did you get a look at the occupants of the car?" Albert asked.

Claire shook her head. "No, it happened too fast."

Later, when she and Albert got to her old convertible on the floor above she was relieved to find that there were no envelopes or notes of any kind clasped under the windshield wipers. Thank God for that! After reporting the near hit and run incident to the police they drove off, with him behind the steering wheel once more, cruising smoothly for the most part except for a minor traffic jam they encountered near the freeway entrance to Interstate 280.

Claire was still shaking a little, with goose bumps on her skin, from what had just occurred, trying to calm her nerves by closing her eyes and meditating a little.

During a traffic light stop before they got on the freeway, Albert gently put his hand on her forearm and caressed it. "You okay, babe?"

"Uh-huh," she replied, even though she really wasn't but didn't want to talk about it. At least not now.

Later, they reached her apartment across the bay, where she quickly grabbed her phone charger and things, before they took off again. She didn't notice anything weird or unusual at her place aside from the fact they it was very quiet and still, without even a murmur or peep from her surrounding neighbors. Which was weird in itself because her neighbors weren't that quiet.

CHAPTER NINE

Robert stood before the assembled congregation, all of them dressed in black hooded robes, looking at him attentively and eagerly. A couple of them even stood slightly bowed, hands clasped tightly together, as if they were in prayer or worship. The latter was probably closer to the truth, for Robert sometimes viewed himself as a god or deity…okay, okay, *most* of the time. Let's spit it out. No need to hide it or beat around the bush now. He was a star, a savior, a messiah, a revolutionary, a rebel, and yes, a *god*. No need to be modest now. Modesty certainly wasn't a quality he would use to describe himself.

"This coven is hereby convened on this twentieth day of September," Robert said, wearing a black hooded robe himself. "Thank you for attending and thank you for your continued commitment, allegiance, and loyalty to the Almighty Lord of Darkness." He looked away from the podium briefly, glancing down at a large pentagram that had been imprinted on the ground a few inches to his left. Lit black candles circled around the inverted star. To the left of the pentagram was a small marble altar and resting on the surface of it was a steel animal cage with a rooster inside of it.

"Brothers and sisters, we are gathered here tonight to offer a special harvest sacrifice to our Almighty Lord of Darkness," Robert continued, looking at each member of the coven. "A gift which is a symbol of our deep and utmost appreciation and love to our Almighty Lord."

The members of the coven started chanting softly.

Robert looked up, his eyes searching the depths of the heavens imploringly. "Oh, Almighty Lord, please accept our gift and in return please protect and shield us from thy enemies who wish to destroy us and our mission. That mission, that goal, of advancing the white race and protecting and treasuring our sacred culture from the numerous undesirables and dregs of society. From that vile filth, the mud people, that are quickly encroaching on our lands and driving us from said lands that rightfully belong to us. Long before the indigenous tribes laid a stake on this holy and fertile soil was the white man, the white race. Yes, brothers and sisters, you heard right! That's not ear wax blocking your hearing. We were here first before the Indians were...and then this land was *stolen* from us, yanked and ripped away from us, and then plundered and pillaged by those same undesirables." Robert nodded his head emphatically to prove the point and drive the nail home as if it were God's honest truth, as he knew it really was. No bullshit here. Pure as the driven goddamn snow. That truth was speaking through him right now. His heart was pumping like a jackhammer, feeling like it was going to burst out of his chest any second now and his face was all hot and sweaty as he spoke.

"Please protect us, Almighty Lord of Darkness," Robert resumed confidently. "And provide us with a sacred land which the white race can live on and thrive on, *separately*, and away from those other harmful races. This coven awaits your reply, Almighty Lord."

A moment later, after he had caught his breath and regained his composure, Robert held up a photo of Claire Goldman, held it up high, for all the coven members to see. Held it up high to make a mockery of her, to show what a despicable person she was.

He frowned and said, "And *this*, brothers and sisters, *this* vile and harmful woman is continuing to spread lies and misconceptions about the mission and values that we uphold so dearly in our lives. In her book, she openly attacks our organization and others like it with extreme hostility and prejudice." Robert paused to let that important point sink in, looking each member in the eyes. "She *must* be stopped before she destroys us all completely. Before everything we stand for and believe in is annihilated from the face of this planet." Robert stared up at the ceiling again, hypnotized, his mind charged with a natural high, fervor, and delirium he had not experienced before, with his hands raised up in the air this time as if he were striving to reach up to those sacred skies. "Dear Almighty Lord, please give us the strength and fortitude to conquer and slay thy enemies, please, Almighty Lord...*please* acknowledge us. We await your response."

Moments later, he flipped open a large, well-thumbed tome on the podium and began reading some passages aloud in Latin.

* * *

"So what do you think of my book?" Claire asked, rubbing her bare feet as she sat Indian-style on one end of his living room sofa, bundled up in a black bathrobe.

Albert, sitting next to her, considered her question carefully before crafting his response. "In one word?" He paused, adding a little to the suspense.

She started getting impatient, shifting in her seat. "Awwww, c'mon, c'mon, let the cat out of the bag already, will ya?!" she said. Scant traces of her New York accent evident in her voice. It seemed to slip out, or relapse, when she was undergoing periods of high stress or anxiety. "This isn't rocket science or brain surgery." When he continued with his deliberations, she sighed, shook her head pitifully, and added: "All right, drum roll, please!" She played air drums, counting down the seconds.

He cleared his throat theatrically, like some snobbish and pretentious book reviewer, before answering: "Okay, three words," he amended. "Concise, detailed, and preachy."

"*Preachy?* she protested.

"You asked for my opinion on your work," he replied calmly. "There it is."

Claire, still taken aback, turned and looked at him. "*Preachy?*" she repeated.

"Just my two-cents, for what it's worth, which may be nothing at all," he said, raising his hands up in the air harmlessly. "Take it with a grain of salt. It's not the be-all-and-end-all review you're going to get for the book. Look at the praise and accolades you've garnered so far. You should be proud of those. So far, they outnumber the negative reviews...and don't forget that sales have been good and steady up to this point."

She scratched his back tenderly. "All the more reason not to strangle you, hon," she purred sensually in his ear before kissing and nibbling it.

"And just out of curiosity, how many reviewers have actually used the word '*preachy*' to describe the book?"

She shrugged. "Oh, I don't know...and I don't care. You're the only one that counts in my book." Scratching his back again.

Albert ruminated on the subject matter with more thought. "And *who'd* be serious and crazy enough to want to kill you just because it's preachy?"

"The sixty-four thousand dollar question," Claire answered. "With added inflation, cost of living adjustments, taxes, and hidden fees, of course."

* * *

Before leaving his apartment, Robert deftly composed an email on his computer. He leaned forward on his elbows, reading the email aloud to himself to make sure it sounded right before clicking on the **Send** button. The email went like this: '*Dear Brothers and Sisters, the day of the big rally is almost upon us, one of the most crucial and important events of our lifetime and perhaps this generation. What's at stake here is the future and survival of our race, of our ideals and our dreams and desires. Your attendance at this very critical and important event is vital. Without your invaluable participation, input, and feedback there* *would be no Utopia Euro-West and the current and future state of affairs for the white race would also be nonexistent and we'd be hurled to the wolves, quite frankly. Need I say more? The permits for the venue space have been secured and the funding has also been guaranteed. All you have to do now is simply show up, Brothers and Sisters. I look forward to seeing you all next week.*

Thank you and Godspeed,

Robert Van Hess

President and Founder of Utopia Euro-West'

He glanced at the clock. 5:57 P.M. Time to get moving and get business taken care of. He stood up, shrugged into his coat which matched the rest of his charcoal-colored Brooks Brother suit, collected his wallet, phone, and keys from his nightstand and headed straight to the door.

The walk to the local pub took less than twenty minutes and when he arrived there was a vacant stool awaiting him at the polished mahogany bar.

He nodded at the bartender. "Good evening. Greyhound, please."

"Coming right up," the bartender replied.

A minute or two later, a man clad entirely in black stood next to him at the bar. Aside from the man's pale white skin which resembled fine, smooth clay and his jet-black hair, like it had been neatly brushed on with a paintbrush, there was nothing else remarkable or outstanding about him.

Without even turning his head or his eyes, Robert muttered, "Goths and tardiness. Some things never change."

The bartender returned a moment later with his drink.

"Cheers," Robert said. "What's your poison tonight, Jeremy? My treat."

"Whiskey," the man clad in black replied.

"Bartender," Robert said, placing the order. Then he turned his attention back to Jeremy. "How's the antique book business these days?"

"Slow. Not much interest in rare manuscripts, I'm afraid. I read a recent study that revealed less than fifty percent of Americans read one book per month."

"There you have it, the dumbing down of America," Robert declared pitifully, taking a sip of his drink. "Everybody's glued to their phones, frying their pathetic brains out."

Jeremy's whiskey arrived and he saluted him and said, "Cheers to the rise of America's new savior, Utopia Euro-West, who will save us all from destruction."

Robert clinked his glass against Jeremy's, nodding sagely. "Amen to that, brother. Along with the cockroaches, the white man and the white woman is all that's gonna be left on this God forsaken planet and we're gonna be stuck to clean the shit off the streets. Just you wait and see, brother."

"Based on what that study indicated, I believe you." Because of the loud noise inside the pub, he stepped closer to Robert, raising his voice a little. "I presume that you are fully prepared for next week's event."

He turned and looked Jeremy dead in the eye, serious as a heart attack. "Is my name Robert or what?"

Jeremy grinned slyly. "I was stupid to ask, my bad."

"You know me, brother, my attention to detail is impeccable as always," Robert stated flat out and center, for the official record, for the whole world to hear and witness. Remember, modesty would *not* be a word used to describe him at all. He could care less about what other people thought. Fuck them! Utopia Euro-West was here to stay. Screw the naysayers, the critics, and the liberal and progressive left. Screw Claire Goldman and her fucking book! After the smoke and ashes cleared from the apocalypse all that would be left would be those damn roaches and the white race. End of story.

Robert stared at him fixedly. "Question is, brother, are *you* ready for the rally?" A hardcore, do-or-die question for the cause. "How far will you go for us, brother?" He expected he knew Jeremy's answer before the words would even leave his mouth, at least he thought he'd know, based on his relationship with him. And he'd known him for a while now.

Jeremy returned that same crazed and obsessed stare, the one that would be frozen and imprinted on his face when he lay dying for the white race. "*Seriously?* You need to ask *me* that?"

Robert grinned ear-to-ear when he heard his response.

CHAPTER TEN

The following week, final preparations were being made for the rally; the big spectacle. Much hype and buzz surrounded the event, elevating it to be one of the most trended and searched topics on the Internet in recent weeks. Much of what had contributed to that was the aura of mystery and controversy generated by the organization behind the event, Utopia Euro-West. Initially, the group's roots were humble and enigmatic, not generating more than a blip in the news, but over the course of time they organically grew bigger and bigger to the point where they were now maintaining steady membership enrollment, accepting donations from people, and making consistent appearances on talk shows, radio, podcasts, magazines, and talks and rallies on the college lecture circuit. In fact, each time that Robert completed a university lecture they would get an immediate spike in membership without fail (he honestly could not remember the last time when no one signed up after he spoke, that's how positive the numbers had been recently), with students whipping out their phones and jumping on the group's website or social media pages to join or post praiseworthy comments and rants about what they had just witnessed and heard at his talk. For them it was like experiencing the second coming of Jesus Christ or something. "Oh, Lord, I see the light!" Robert recalled one participant raving at one of his talks. "It was phenomenal!" somebody would remark. "Jaw dropping", "Deep", others would comment. He'd literally leave audiences breathless, in awe, sobbing, electrified, and wanting more, more, and more.

And so help me God, I will deliver the goods, Robert thought. *Or may lightning strike me down! I live to communicate the message of the cause to the hungry and curious masses.*

And what was inherently wrong with the content of the message? Absolutely nothing. *Screw the haters!* There was nothing illegal or criminal about it as far as he could see. *And*, he had freedom of speech on his side. Thank the Lord! He had every right to voice his opinion, to speak his mind, as any other red-blooded American living on this soil. Look at Black Lives Matter. They were utilizing freedom of speech. Goody good for them and good luck to them. *Works both ways, brother. You work up a frenzy and advocate for your own race and I'll do the same for mine. Amen.*

Robert knew a fellow who belonged to the National Association for the Advancement of White People and the guy imparted some words of wisdom to him which he still adhered and subscribed to to this day: "One does not have or create enemies until he or she is provoked, humiliated, harassed, and attacked. But even then they are not enemies in the true sense of the word. They are just obstacles and challenges that one needs to overcome to reach his or her goal. When you say or do something with the utmost conviction and confidence, whatever it is, people will listen and respond. Once you achieve that you can tackle anything in life."

Now Robert, more than ever, was ready to deliver the latest message from his organization to that information and knowledge hungry crowd who were ready to devour it up and stand alongside him and his cause.

He stood before the bathroom mirror, looking at his reflection for a moment, and admiring his blonde "Fashy Haircut". Gazing back into those pure blue eyes of his. Robert, sly silver tongue that he was, could still woo the girls and make 'em swoon for they always fell and got weak in the knees for those baby blues of his. He nodded at himself before abruptly breaking out into a truly wicked grin.

"Ladies and gentlemen," he began theatrically as though he was on live TV. "It's show time."

* * *

Claire finished writing her comments in red ink on the right-hand margin of the paper, topping it off by putting a large **A** at the very top and circling it. She then tossed the paper on the mountainous heap of ones that she had already corrected before grabbing the next one from her to do pile. She glanced at the clock and yawned. The house was deathly silent. Still no Albert. His last afternoon class had ended at four-thirty and he should've been home by now…although…wait…didn't he say he was going to the gym straight after work? Oh, that's right, he did. She tossed her red pen on the table, took off her glasses, and leaned back against the chair, massaging her eyelids and forehead. Boy, her brain and eyes were fried! It had been a long day. Her eyes seriously needed a break now after having stared at all those pages and pages of student papers for the past few hours. Deadlines did that to you. She was grateful that deadlines kept everything organized and in check but at the same time they made her body all tense and achy, and her posture bad from all that sitting.

Ahhh! Which now quickly prompted her to get her butt off the chair, stand up, and walk over to the living room to do some stretches. The two exchange students were there, quietly sitting on the couch. The guy with his laptop on his lap, ear-buds plugged in both ears and his eyes gazing intently on the screen, and the woman alternating back and forth between reading a textbook and jotting down notes on her pad. They didn't notice her come in.

Claire thought it best to make some sort of greeting, mainly out of kindness and courtesy, but also so they wouldn't be startled by her sudden appearance. She smiled and simply said, "Good evening."

At first there was only silence for she didn't think they heard her, certainly not the young man who had tuned everything else out by the looks of it...his name was Lee, wasn't it? Usually she was good with the names of her own students...yeah, that was it. But also, Claire figured they did not hear her because she didn't say it loud enough for they were busy studying and she didn't want to look like a lame ass raising her voice and all.

Claire tried again, just a tad bit louder this time, and said, "Good evening."

This time the Asian woman looked all around the living room, trying to figure out where Claire's voice was coming from and when she finally saw her, her eyes widened a little as she noticed Claire for the first time.

Lee looked up from his laptop and saw her, too, removing his ear-buds.

Claire maintained her friendly but sheepish grin. "Sorry, didn't mean to interrupt your studying! Just wanted to say hello, that's all." She stepped closer to them, extending her hand. "Hi, I'm Claire…Albert's friend." She had debated using the word, *girlfriend*, instead but figured they pretty much got the picture, or that Albert had maybe mentioned her in passing or something. Surely, he must've said something about having a friend staying over or perhaps the students had already put two and two together when they saw all her personal belongings in boxes and bags the day she moved in.

Lee was the first one who jolted up (a sign of good etiquette and upbringing already), stepped over, and accepted her hand, shaking it. "Hello, I am Lee." He gestured to the woman. "This is Pei."

Claire immediately wondered if they were dating, or whether they were just friends, or if they even knew each other at all, and then quickly cast aside those trivial thoughts. She shook Pei's hand as well, noticing her handshake was limp and weak. *Not a good sign!* You can tell a lot about someone by their handshake.

Pei nodded and smiled at her. "Nice meeting you."

"Nice meeting you, too," Claire replied, glancing down at her textbook. "Ahh, an anthropology major." She looked at Lee. "You as well?"

"Yes," he answered.

"Oh, that makes sense," Claire rationalized. "That's why Albert is hosting you, being that he is a teacher in the same department. Are you taking any of his courses this semester?"

"Yes," Lee repeated. "We're both taking two of his classes."

"Albert's a good teacher," Claire added for good measure. "Of course, it's hard for me to be objective about that since I'm his friend."

Lee softened up a little more, grinning. "You are correct. He is very knowledgeable about the subject of anthropology. Very detail oriented."

Claire nodded. "That he is."

"And he is a good speaker," Pei interjected, from where she sat on the sofa.

Claire nodded again. "I'll give him that as well. Well, I'll let you two get back to studying. Nice chatting with you."

Lee grinned again and said, "Nice talking to you, too."

Claire went to the kitchen, filled the tea kettle with some water, put it on the stove, and turned on the burner. She sat down on one of the straight back wooden chairs at the kitchen table, leaned back, took a deep breath, and took stock of where she, Claire Goldman, was at right now. Why was she living at Albert's house now? Well, because of the letters, the threats, of course. But she felt like it was such an imposition on him, felt like she was cramping and taking up his space, his style, invading his territory, so to speak, especially with the students here as well. Personal space was scarce as it was. But he kept insisting, many times, that he did not mind her living here temporarily, that he was completely okay with it, and that he wanted her here because he wanted to protect her and wanted to keep her safe. He wouldn't lie about that. She could tell when he was lying.

Now what about the two of them being in a romantic relationship again? How did Claire *truly* feel about that? *Be blunt and honest now.* He had brought it up earlier and the question came up: '*You mean being a couple again or getting married again?*' Honestly speaking, she was completely fine about being in a relationship with Albert again. In fact, she was loving it now. She was happy and couldn't honestly recall being happier and content like this in so many years. It felt like they were both having a second wind of sorts with romance and picking up exactly where they had left off, resuming things after that divorce so many moons ago. Being with Albert now brought back a rush of so many memories of the past, of the old college days, of New York City. Being with him now rekindled and re-solidified that old romance. As far as tying the knot with him once more she wasn't sure...*I mean, does it even matter at this point?* Really. It's only an official piece of paper declaring that they were an official item again, that's all. They both knew in their hearts' heart that they loved each other very much and knew how they felt about one another. Did they really need that official document to validate that? It's not like they were a young couple fresh out of college who were ready to get engaged, get hitched, and all that...but still, the thought and concept of marriage was nice, noble, and romantic in itself. It proved chivalry, old-school values, and traditions still existed in this world...but if Albert really wanted to go through the whole process again, if he really wanted to go through the motions, of jumping through the hoops of getting married once more, she supposed she could be swayed. It would show that he was still truly in love with her, that he really cared about her, and that he would support and compliment her no matter what.

She took another deep breath, massaging her forehead. *Now what about this business with the death threats?* How did she deal with that issue? How could it be resolved? Should she continue fleeing and escaping from the threat? She didn't want to keep living in fear, of having to look over her shoulder all the time, of having to cower and be timid. No, that's no quality of life. With all her training and background in feminist studies and being an advocate and activist for rape victims, her gut instinct told her to fight back and stand her ground. And that's what she intended to do now, and not be forced to run away from the problem.

The sound of the tea kettle whistling, sounding almost like it was shrieking, woke her up from her internal dialogue with herself and brought her back to the present moment. After turning off the stove and pouring the hot water in a cup, she added the green tea bag and let it sit and steep for a bit. She was sitting there in the chair contemplating her mental checklist, which included at the very top, prepping for an anti-rape, self-defense workshop for women as well as an orientation for new volunteers at the rape crisis hotline, all on the same weekend, by the way, when suddenly she heard the front door of the house open and slam shut...then heard Albert's voice, the timber and pitch lower than it usually was, maybe due to the fact that he had a long day at work and an exhausting work out at the gym, as he checked in and chatted with Lee and Pei.

A few moments later, he stood leaning against the kitchen's door frame, his eyelids droopy, suppressing a yawn, as he shot her a tired but heartfelt grin, his dark hair still damp from a recent shower and the sleeves of his dress shirt rolled up to his elbows.

"Hey," Claire said, immediately rising and walking over to where he stood and embracing him with a tight, warm hug, and which culminated with her delivering a quick peck to his lips. "It was getting late and I was worried about you, wondering where you were. And then I remembered you were going to the gym after work." She looked up at him, peering into his eyes that looked like they were going to drop shut at any second, patting his butt playfully. "You better get to bed, sleepy head! Long day for you, babe."

"Uhm-hmmm!" he replied, leaning down a little to graze and lick her ear sensually with his warm tongue. And then ran his tongue teasingly and passionately along her neck. The room began to get real hot all of a sudden.

She smiled. "Gettin' a second wind there, are you, sailor?"

"Uhm-hmmm!" he repeated, grabbing her shapely, heart-shaped buttocks and massaging them tenderly, lovingly, and slowly with his hands, and *teasingly*, as if he was kneading dough, trying to wet, build up, and arouse her sexual appetite.

Well, whatever his mojo or magic was, it was growing on her and it was working just fine. And a lot of it had to do, in large part, because of those magic hands of his. *Wow!* was all she could think of right now, as she allowed herself to be enchanted, seduced, and escorted back to his bedroom in the back of the house. *There goes my tea!* she thought, catching one last glimpse of the cup on the kitchen table, with curls of steam still rising up from it, before being led away.

"Thank God the students didn't catch us in the middle of all that!" she whispered to him. "We've gotta be more discreet next time."

He smiled it off as he held her tight, his *magic hands* sliding underneath her panties, and exploring the hidden pleasures down there. Oh, well, so much for being exhausted after a good work out.

* * *

Midway through the orientation and training for the new volunteers at the rape crisis hotline's office on Sunday, Claire, standing before the large group, one of the biggest volunteer trainings they had in a while, grabbed the mouse and clicked out of the slideshow presentation that she showed them earlier that morning. She then stepped from the laptop over to a large, old-school TV sitting on a metal rack with wheels attached to it, popped a disc into the DVD player on another rack below it, and stabbed the **Play** button with her finger. Seconds later, after some hissing sounds and visual fuzziness disappeared, a title appeared on the TV screen: **Rape 101 Basics: Myths and Facts**

When the hissing noises and video glitches resurfaced several seconds later, she said, "Sorry, folks. Please bear in mind that this documentary was made in the eighties and I had this transferred from a VHS tape, and though it's dated in spots, the information presented is still pretty good and useful. After it's finished we'll have a brief discussion about the program before breaking for lunch."

Claire dimmed the lights in the conference room, and while the group members looked at the screen with rapt attention, she quietly stepped out of the room and strode down a hallway to her office. After retrieving her cell phone from her desk she checked it for messages. Two text messages from Albert. The first one read:

'Just thinking of you…wish you were home with me now. I miss you already…last night with you was fucking amazing as always! Lying in bed now and wishing you were here right beside me to keep me warm. I slept in this morning, am reading the paper in bed now with my perfunctory cup of coffee on the nightstand…okay, I'll let you go now 'cause I know you've got a full plate with that training today. I'll come pick you up when it's over and we can grab dinner at that new vegetarian restaurant you've been wanting to check out. See you soon.

Love always,
Albert'

Claire smiled, moving on to his second text, which was a GIF of a giant red heart with a message below it that said, 'I can't stop thinking about you! It feels magical when I'm with you.' She maintained her grin as she pecked out a reply to him that said: 'Hey, you're the one with the magical hands!'

A few seconds later, his reply popped up on the screen: an emoji with a mischievous grin. She smiled before putting away her phone and then headed for the restroom. After checking herself out in the mirror for a moment, touching up her '80s-style mullet a little bit, and applying some lotion to her face and lips, she spun on her heel, ready to go into one of the stalls when all of a sudden, from out of nowhere, she saw a tall man dressed entirely in black standing there in one corner of the restroom. Watching her very intently, like a big cat studying its prey. She could feel his eyes drilling themselves into her skull. His slicked back, jet-black hair matched his black clothing perfectly and seamlessly. *Where the hell did he come from?! Did he just step through the walls like a ninja???* She could've swore this room, supposedly a sacred and sanctified space for females only, and located in the offices of a rape crisis hotline center, no less, had been empty a minute ago.

Claire almost jumped out of her own skin, screaming. "Get out!" she bellowed. "You're *not* allowed in here!"

The man, his face as stoic and impassive as stone, ignored her, walking towards her.

She immediately turned to run, getting as far as the door, but was not able to grab the handle to open it, for he was much faster and cunning than her, his height and long legs giving him the advantage of long, runner's strides in which he was able to close the gap between them in two wide strides.

He snatched her up like she weighed nothing at all and slammed her against the wall adjacent to the sinks, with such violent and brute force that she felt her teeth rattle and saw bright stars flashing before her. Her back exploded in pain, feeling a minor crack in the wall as well. But despite the electric currents of pain that rippled throughout her body, despite the headache that felt like it would slice her brain in two, she punched and kicked him with as much strength as she could possibly muster. Stomping him hard on the foot with her boots, which made him wince and grunt. In fact, Claire tried to utilize as many as the rape self-defense tactics she had taught her volunteers and students over the years. She even delivered a partially successful kick to the guy's nuts, a true-and-tried favorite, but her foot did not connect all the way as she had hoped it would, for he possessed enough quick reflexes and instincts to block it.

Such a shame, too, for Claire thought if it had connected one hundred percent it would've immobilized the man and given her some time to flee. But this guy was a pro, he knew what he was doing for he had probably done it lots of times to other women and men. He wasn't messing around for he had that determined gaze in his eyes. Like nothing was going to stop him.

Right now, she just wanted to be able to survive this encounter and live another day. She tried to push him off of her but he was bigger, had more mass, and was much stronger than her. She kicked and thrashed her body against his, but to no avail. The black clad man simply held her frame up against the wall, pinning her arms tight against the wall like she was some helpless cow ready to be slaughtered. He was standing so close to her now that she caught whiffs of his rank and foul breath; it was as if he hadn't brushed his teeth in days or weeks.

Before Claire could resist or put up much more of a fight, for she certainly felt she still had lots of juice inside of her to ward him off, he hit her viciously in the face, a boxer's severe and lethal sucker punch, sheer, lightning-fast velocity and energy, leaving her no time to react and think, and suddenly she was staring at nothing but bright stars again before her whole world crashed and faded to black and she went limp.

The last thought that crossed her mind, two thoughts, actually, before she went out were: *The volunteers...they'll be waiting for me after the video is finished...and...and...and...Albert will be coming later to pick me up...Albert...*

CHAPTER ELEVEN

She didn't know how long she'd been out cold.

It could've been half an hour, an hour, four hours, a day, or maybe more…she had absolutely no clue whatsoever. What she did know, and what she was very conscious and aware of at the moment, was the splitting migraine headache she was suffering from, it was a downright killer. Hands down, the worst one she'd ever had. And she definitely had her fair share of migraines all throughout her life, including some real winners back in her college heyday when she was studying like mad, cramming and cramming and staying up late, occasionally drinking and partying on the weekends and paying the price for all that fun the day after. But this current migraine was the crown jewel of them all, making the others pale in comparison, and she had to thank the black clad man for that. Jesus, he had a nasty swing! When he hit her, she kept thinking: *This is it: I'm going to die, I'm going to die now.* Her life about to flash by her very eyes. And she knew he must be a white nationalist. In fact, she'd bet her life or her next paycheck on it. Maybe from Utopia Euro-West, maybe from another group, but she knew he was one of *them* for sure. He had that sheen and overall look about him. The guy looked like a mercenary from one of those old-school dime store detective novels. Black leather trench coat, black T-shirt, black leather pants, and black leather, steel-toe boots. The only thing missing from him was a semiautomatic assault rifle. And no, she did not know the guy, had never seen him before. For all she knew he might just be a hired gun, so to speak, and not one of the administrative or core members of the group...how she'd kill for some Tylenol or medication now to alleviate this frickin' headache.

The other thing that Claire realized was that her face felt all puffy and swollen and she felt dried blood caked on the rim of her nostrils as well as on her lips. She winced when her fingers ran across that swollen part of her face, the part that had been struck by that guy's fist, for it felt like she was touching the countenance of the Elephant Man or something! It felt vastly different from what her face normally felt like. Wait until she found a mirror and saw the ultimate truth. She'd probably have a frickin' heart attack when she did. Her nose did not feel broken, at least not from the naked touch, but she didn't know for certain...and her back...oh, brother, did it hurt! Every time she moved it felt like razor sharp knives were stabbing into her back and spine. *Ouch!*

As far as where she physically was, location wise, from what she could gather and gauge, she was lying on her side on the floor with her wrists and ankles bound together with heavy duty duct tape, and she was still clothed and did not appear to have been physically or sexually violated or assaulted. The operative words here were, 'did not appear.' Claire breathed a small sigh of relief for that, for things could have been much, much worse than they were now...things could have ended very badly indeed for her. She could've been left for dead, dismembered or mutilated and dumped in the boonies…and the place she was in now…it was…the size of an outhouse, only a little bigger, but it certainly smelled like one…*ooooooooh, did it ever! The stink of this space!* She coughed several times and held her breath every now and then.

Air! she thought. *I need air! When are they gonna let me out of here?!*

She tried to wrestle free from the restraints but it seemed totally futile for she felt glued together by the duct tape. Well, at least she was not gagged…at least she could breathe, if you can call breathing stinky air breathing at all.

Several seconds later, Claire heard movement…footsteps outside the outhouse's door. Faint at first, but gradually growing more audible by the second. Oddly enough, the door handle of the room was shaped like a wheel, resembling one for a submarine or some retro government research facility. She watched as that wheel turned, accompanied by a loud, squeaky sound that she expected it to be associated with.

When the door finally opened, the black clad man entered silently, that same stoic, impassive expression on his pale white face, which resembled smooth clay. Claire cringed when he approached her and knelt down beside her.

"I demand you release me right now!" she said, but it sounded a little silly to her at the moment for some reason, maybe because she knew he wouldn't oblige her request. "You've committed a crime and will be prosecuted to the full extent of the law, you know that, don't you?"

The man's facial expression didn't change in the slightest, as if he hadn't heard her at all. She was talking to a wall.

"It's illegal to hold me here," she added for good measure, knowing that saying something, however foolish or insignificant it may be, advocating for herself basically, was better than remaining silent. She, of all the people in the world, should know that, being a rape crisis advocate and activist. Remaining silent was the killer and the major reason for why rapists remained loose and at large.

Still, no response from the man.

"Say something, goddamnit!" she bellowed, her voice echoing throughout the room. "Don't give me that silent treatment crap!"

The man glanced at her but did not acknowledge her comment.

"*Who are you?*" Claire persisted, eyeing him with disgust, not about to surrender to the jaws of defeat. "What organization do you represent? Who do you answer to?"

Without uttering a single word the black clad man, as if in ninja or stealth mode, delivered a swift, tremendous blow to the side of her face, slamming it to the ground with a thud so hard that it vibrated the very foundation of the room. That thud echoed throughout the small space.

Claire's head lolled to one side of her neck like a lifeless ragged doll. Oh, God, that migraine was worse than ever now and she was gonna puke...oh, jeez, it felt like a tank had rolled over her head...she didn't want to die like this, not this way, and certainly not here in this cesspool...no, Lord, please don't take me yet. I'm not ready...my job isn't finished here on Earth. There's still so much left for me to do. Let me live a little longer so that I can continue to help, educate, and empower those sisters in need, the ones that are still being oppressed and physically and verbally assaulted by this patriarchal society. Allow me to continue to be one of your agents and advocates of change, a messenger of the revolution...give me some more time so that I can properly say goodbye to my family, friends, and to Albert. The last thing she saw before she lost consciousness was that black clad man glaring down at her like she was some bug that he needed to squash.

* * *

Albert had started worrying the moment that Claire did not respond to his text message for she always replied back, like clockwork, no matter what. It was totally unlike her to not answer back. Even a simple one liner or one word text from her would've put him at ease. And ever since they began seeing one another again they had called and texted each other daily, without fail or interruption...so this delay, this void of silence, was definitely strange and a cause for concern.

When she did not reply to his second text, one regarding his estimated time of arrival to pick her up and to inform her that the new vegetarian restaurant she wanted to try was actually closed today due to unforeseen circumstances, he really grew anxious and started pacing in circles. Maybe it was time to call the police. Albert called her five times in a row, getting her voicemail each and every single time. *C'mon, Claire, answer the damn phone!* Who he called next was the rape crisis hotline office itself but he was put on hold for what seemed like an eternity, having to endure listening to cloying elevator muzak. He finally hung up, sighing in frustration, when no one returned to the line. Next he dialed the number of one of her close colleagues at the university who may have an idea of Claire's whereabouts but got her voicemail instead and hung up. After that, Albert contacted the people in her life such as her parents and family members, asking them if they'd heard from her or spoke to her but none of them had.

Okay, this isn't leading anywhere, he thought, and finally decided to just drive out to the offices of the rape crisis hotline and hope to find her there. Maybe she had just stepped out for a second, to grab some fresh air after being cooped up indoors for a training for so long, or to take a walk around the building to clear her head as she was prone to do when she needed space or time to think. That was his sweetie, yeah, he could picture her doing those things. Or maybe she had to field an urgent call, one where she needed some privacy and left the building temporarily. Yeah, that's it right there...now stop worrying, would ya?

When he arrived at the hotline's office some thirty minutes later, no thanks to the sluggish, stop-and-go traffic to Oakland, he was buzzed inside by a staff member who greeted him with a grave frown on her face. *Oh shit! No!* His stomach sank immediately and his heartbeat accelerated as soon as he saw her facial expression for he figured Claire was injured or dead. Take your pick. But in light of her new book and the death threats it wouldn't be a complete shocker. Deep down inside he knew something bad was going to happen to her. It was just a matter of time. It was inevitable. A time bomb just waiting to explode. He couldn't protect her every single minute of the day.

When he was with the staff member, he cut straight to the chase and asked her, "Where's Claire?"

"She's missing," the staff member replied.

His anxieties and sadness quickly disappeared, replaced by feelings of hope and optimism, causing him to jump a little, giving him a little spring of life and salvation, and almost even causing him to smile in elation. *She's not dead!! She's not dead!! Thank you, God! Thank you!* He breathed a sigh of relief, trying to appear calm now.

"Any idea where she may be?" he asked quickly. "Did she leave a note or anything?"

The staff member shook her head. "You're Albert, right?"

"Yes."

"No, she didn't leave any message for you but she did tell me you were coming to pick her up after the volunteer training was done."

An idea popped up in his head. "May I speak to the volunteers?" he asked.

"Sure." The staff member led him to the conference room where the volunteers were congregated, most of them with sad, gloomy frowns on their faces. Some of them were talking among themselves, and upon his arrival they quickly lowered their voices to whispers, perhaps feeling a little threatened or intimidated by the presence of a man at a rape crisis center. He understood and didn't blame or judge them for that. And after talking to each one of them separately, Albert learned that they were a nice bunch of women who were just as concerned about Claire as he was. That in the brief amount of time that they'd known her they found her to be a very inspiring, genuine, and supportive person. A few mentioned they joined the training because of her and what an icon she was in feminist circles. Some remarked that they admired her bravery in writing that new book, that she had the guts to challenge the conservative right.

But unfortunately, none of the volunteers knew where she may have gone. *Or*, more importantly, who may have abducted her. The last time they all saw her was when she left the conference room as they began watching a video. That was the last time.

"Did anybody notice anything unusual in the office today?" Albert asked. "Did anyone see any suspicious person or people lurking around the premises?"

The staff member shook her head.

"Did the security cameras capture anything?" he persisted.

After he pleaded and insisted, the staff member took him to a tiny back room where the video equipment was located. She played back today's security footage from all the mounted cameras around the office but they did not see any strange or abnormal activity. But that didn't mean it didn't exist, of course.

It simply meant Albert had some digging and snooping around to do, which he enjoyed doing. Being nosy and all and asking a lot of detailed questions. But first and foremost, he called the police and told them what had happened to Claire. It was important to have an official, documented paper trail now. And if he knew the cops, and he think he did somewhat based on the fair amount of interactions he had with them, he knew it would probably take them a while to find her, let alone get started on the case. Point being that they were probably swamped with lots of missing persons cases. He suddenly recalled a remark and criticism Claire had made recently concerning the police department's investigation of the dead cat found in her apartment.

'They've been as slow as molasses,' he remembered her saying. 'Friendly and kind but slow as a snail.'

Which meant she wanted results pronto. At the snap of her fingers speed. Albert told her that type of expectation wasn't realistic considering how many cases of burglary, break-ins, and vandalism the Oakland PD received. 'You've gotta be patient, babe,' he told her. 'It's a process and you're in a queue like everything else in life.'

Claire wasn't the patient type, unfortunately, and wanted things her way all the time. She wasn't like that all the time, of course. She'd learn and get used to it.

The voice of the staff member pulled him back, *dragged* him back (was more like it) to the here and now, from his inner thoughts, which he sometimes easily got entangled in, and steered him back to the conversation at hand.

"Huh?" Albert asked, momentarily lost in a daze, as if trying to navigate his way out of the fog.

The staff member had the patience of Job and had no problem repeating her question. "Would you like me to assist you with anything else?"

"May I look around her office?" he asked. "Just want to see if I can backtrack her last steps before she vanished."

"Sure, let me show you where it's at," she replied, and guided him down a stylish, bluish-gray colored corridor past a series of open doorways, one being the actual crisis hotline room itself, set up with numerous cubicles where a person sat behind a telephone and computer console.

They finally arrived at a spacious-sized room at the end of the hallway with a nameplate on the door that read: **Claire Goldman, Executive Director and Co-Founder**

It had a nice, snazzy ring to it. He liked it. Claire had told him that opening and managing the hotline center was one of the proudest achievements in her career. Definitely one of her highlights, she said. It was her baby, one that she had slaved so hard to get from being a mere idea on a piece of scratch paper to being a fully realized, three dimensional, functioning office inside an actual building. Securing funding, permits, and a patent and trademark for the business were all part of the roller coaster ride that now seemed like a lifetime ago, looking back in hindsight. Albert remembered her talking about wanting to create and build such a place during her early, hardcore feminist activist days at Columbia. She had joked about how it seemed like a pipe dream back then. But look at her now.

Albert thanked the staff member for her time and quickly began searching around Claire's desk for anything that might provide clues as to her whereabouts. He saw her cell phone sitting on the large desk calendar on the middle of the desk and picked it up.

Why did she leave this behind? he thought, touching the screen and seeing the wallpaper of him and Claire holding hands at the beach on it. It asked for a password and he tried to remember if she had told him what it was. *Shoot, I don't think she told me, at least I don't recall her telling me.* Albert pocketed the phone anyway and continued perusing through the drawers of the desk, flipping through notebooks, her day planner, and file folders.

Nothing.

He looked through her purse and wallet. Nothing. No money missing. Why would she leave that behind? It was starting to look more and more like a kidnapping and not her going somewhere on her own free will.

Next, he looked through items on a nearby bookshelf but didn't find anything particularly helpful. A file cabinet parallel to the desk was locked. Probably confidential client information. The desktop computer was also locked as well, requiring a login name and password.

Okay, so he was finished with her office and moved out into the corridor and looked around, trying to deduce where her next steps may have taken her. Where would her abductors have taken her? Looking straight ahead, just down the hallway, he could see the nameplate on a door that said: **Women**. In his mind he could see Claire walking down the corridor to use the restroom.

After checking to make sure no one was inside he entered the women's restroom and quickly took a peek around. No useful clues in any of the stalls, he even rummaged through the garbage can but saw nothing...where else should he look? Could Claire have accidentally dropped something in here? That was quite possible...where though? Hmmm...wait a second! From the corner of his eye he saw a dark object in the stall on the left, lying on one side of the toilet at an angle, almost behind it. Like someone had accidentally dropped it there. No wonder he missed it during his first gander, it was almost obscured from view.

He went inside the stall, squatted down, and reached over to pick up the black matchbook, with all its matchsticks intact except one, interestingly enough. On the front cover of the booklet was a human skull wearing a Nazi-style, World War Two helmet. Beneath the skull were the words: **Castle Blitzkrieg**. And under that was the address of what sounded like a bar.

Albert frowned. *What is this doing inside a women's restroom at a rape crisis hotline center of all places? A white supremacist bar? Seriously?* It was the last thing he'd expect to find in here. Claire certainly would not have left that in here. Definitely fishy. In his mind he could imagine the sort of person that would frequent that type of establishment. It was terrifying to know they were able to infiltrate this office. She wasn't safe anywhere.

* * *

Claire gradually opened her eyes.

The first thing she saw was the semi-darkness of the filthy outhouse. And it was the first thing that she smelled, too. *Yuck!* She was still bound and stuck here. And fortunately, still clothed, too, and still *not* sexually violated, it appeared. Being a rape crisis advocate she was always aware of that. She felt saliva drooling down her chin and wished she could've wiped it off but she couldn't because her wrists were taped together. When she raised her torso a little and looked down she saw that a tiny pool of saliva and blood had collected below her head. She could imagine herself drooling when she was asleep earlier.

How long have I been out? She had no clue, having lost all track of time...and that migraine. It was still there. Not as intense and prominent as before but it was still there. She thought that second vicious blow that he delivered, that sucker punch, was going to be the killer be-all-and-end-all punch. Shit, it certainly felt like it...it felt like her skull had been fractured in half by those two hits...it all happened in the blink of an eye it seemed...she hadn't seen his fist coming at all. Couldn't pull away or duck or anything. Next thing she knew her world had exploded and she saw nothing but pitch blackness and bright stars *BAM!* When his fist connected with her face it seemed like time had stood still for several seconds and all she sensed was the impact of that hit. *POW!* She remembered it sounded like a loud pop.

Well, I've got news for you, pal, I'm still alive and kicking. For the moment, at least. Claire heard her own labored, wheezy breathing. Her face still felt swollen and puffy and probably looked even worse now. Good thing there wasn't a mirror around. *God!* And strangely enough, at this moment, she was angry but not super vindictive, vengeance- seeking angry. Yeah, sure, she *did* want to get even with the guy and avenge what happened to her, and she knew in her heart's heart she'd have her day in court, so to speak, but she was just happy and grateful to still be breathing, quite frankly. *Thank you, Lord.* But Claire realized she may not be so lucky the next time he punched her.

It was right there and then that she realized she wanted to live and see another day with Albert. That she wanted to laugh, giggle, smile, and act silly and loving with him again, again, and again...that she missed him dearly even though they hadn't been apart for more than a day. It was right there and then that she knew she had to find a way to get the fuck out of here...and be able to make that leap to be with him again. She suddenly wondered where he was right now, what he was doing at the moment...was he looking for her? Had he rounded up a posse with bloodhounds to go searching for her?

Claire tried to sit up but a spasm of unrelenting, ruthless pain stabbed and electrified her entire body, causing her to wince and yelp in agony. She tried moving again, clamping down and gritting her teeth hard to endure and suffer the pain, to be tough and take it like a real woman, a real warrior, and not act like some chicken shit coward. *C'mon, woman! Don't give me that stupid damsel in distress bullshit! You can do it, warrior woman! C'mon, you can do it! You got this!* She gradually raised her torso, doing it at that slow pace to minimize the pain that threatened to smother and swallow her whole, but it felt like it took every ounce and bit of her moral and physical fiber as well as her mental capacity to try to complete that action...but eventually she was able to achieve it, grunting and groaning in pain. Doing such an action exhausted every shred of her being. *Do it again! C'mon, I know you can do it.* After taking a few deep breaths, she gritted her teeth tightly again and forced herself up, slowly, against the wall and into a sitting position on the floor, grunting like she was taking a massive dump.

You did it! she thought, sighing. *Now how the hell do I lose these restraints?* She looked around everywhere, wild and wide-eyed like a mad and demonically possessed woman, for anything sharp, be it a razor blade that someone may have accidentally dropped, a nail, a paper clip, an eating utensil, a sharp rock, a pen. *Anything. And hurry up, girl! He could be back at any second.* She once watched this YouTube clip where a dude quickly sliced through a thick mesh of packing tape with the aid of just a paper clip. Puncture, puncture, puncture was his tactic. Her eyes frantically scanned the ground for anything at all…searching…and searching…and searching. But she couldn't see very well because of the dimly lit interior. She was on her knees now, peering down at the floor carefully. When she craned her neck over to one corner of the outhouse she almost keeled over in joy and relief, her heartbeat racing, when she finally saw hope and salvation in a single, thin nail lying on the sticky and grimy ground.

Hurry! she reminded herself. *Before the guy returns.*

Claire snatched up the dirty nail, with dark flecks of God knows what encrusted on it, and began trying to puncture the duct tape and realizing just how difficult it was to do that when her wrists were bound tightly together. But goddamnit, she was more determined than ever now to get the hell out of here and survive, to beat this foe, and to overcome the odds stacked against her. *C'mon, you got this!* She turned the nail around in her right hand to get a better grip on the head, and started over, stabbing the tape with a rage and fury that had bottled up inside of her and that had grown and blossomed to overwhelming proportions.

It was working! The nail was piercing the tape. It was taking some time, precious time which she knew she was running out of, but it was working nonetheless. She kept stabbing the tape like a madwoman hell bent on survival, knowing that her very life depended on it. That the man dressed in black would kill her without a doubt if she didn't escape from here. The fact that he didn't respond to any of her questions showed her that he was a ruthless, merciless, and emotionless killing machine. That was his single goal. She was about a third of the way through now, concentrating hard on the task at hand.

Puncture, puncture, puncture! Claire tried to be calm and patient, taking deep breaths, as she repositioned the nail over a patch of the duct tape that she had been unsuccessful in cutting through. She spiked the material hard, with as much strength as she could muster, grunting in the process. Luckily, the nail was sharp enough to slice through the tape. She kept repeating the motion with sheer, blind focus and raw anger, pushing herself to the max, until that whole section was nothing more than tatters and shreds. As a motivating factor, Claire focused on a mental image of the man in black, imagining that the nail was a knife and that he was the tape, and that she was stabbing him over and over again. Relentlessly.

Stab, stab, stab! That was her current motto. *Focus, focus, focus.* And before she knew it, she had managed to cut through the remainder of the tape, watching the final bits and pieces of debris fall to the floor. Claire reached down and ripped off the tape that bound her ankles together.

Free at last!

She quickly rose to her feet, but *too* fast, for she immediately experienced a monster head rush like no other, almost losing her balance and collapsing to the ground. But fortunately, she was able to grab a hold of the wall to steady herself. After reorienting herself and getting her bearings straight, she took a much needed deep breath, a couple of them, actually, before limping her way to the wheel shaped door handle. She placed her hands on the cold steel of the handle and turned it, the loud, squeaky sound startling her, audible enough to wake the dead it seemed. Now she'd better get the heck out of here for she was certain the guy had heard that. Claire yanked the door open and quickly hobbled out of the room, relieved to be breathing cool, fresh air once more.

CHAPTER TWELVE

She limped as fast as she could down the stretch of a dimly lit hallway with a bare, cobweb festooned light bulb hanging from the ceiling. Cracks in the walls as well as the sight of rusty, leaky pipes showed the age and state of dilapidation of this place. Rats scurried back and forth, running into each other as they searched for food. *Where the hell am I?* she wondered, her head still throbbing with a fiery and persistent pain that she did not think could possibly exist. Her right hand instinctively brushed along the side of her face, and the swollen bruises there immediately reminded her that she was far from okay. She felt like a carnival freak. But when mental pictures of the man in black flooded her exhausted mind once again, she pushed herself straight ahead, hobbling quickly towards a pair of dark double doors, with pebble glazed windows on the upper half.

She slammed down on the exit bar as soon as she reached the doors and stumbled out into bright daylight, causing her to squint and raise her hand to shield herself from the light. From the looks of the environment, with its vintage, 1960s-style classroom doors, trough-style water fountain, and retro-style font of the words stenciled on the doors, she figured this to be an abandoned elementary school. Further evidence to support this claim was the sight of the neglected and overgrown crab grass and high weeds on the patch of green right outside the classroom doors. She suddenly had a flashback to her childhood, of lining up for recess in the school playground, of playing dodge ball and getting struck by that red ball, and of sitting in those ugly and uncomfortable classroom desks and chairs so many moons ago.

Don't stop to think! she screamed at herself. *Keep moving on! Go!* She heeded her own advice and limped in the direction of the exit, a cyclone fence gate that had been locked with a big, rusty brown padlock. After looking over her shoulder and not seeing anyone there she scrambled up the fence like an American Gladiator competing in those absurd events they have on reality TV, despite the protestations of her sore and aching body, hopped over the top of the fence, and landed on the concrete sidewalk on the other side.

Now she found herself at the front entrance of the defunct school, with the parking lot devoid of vehicles save for an old school bus, the yellow paint faded and almost bleached white from having spent God knows how many years under the powerful rays of the sun. All the tires of the bus had been slashed. Located next to the school was an open field that appeared like it had been cleared of development many years ago, and ironically it was roughly the size of a high school football field. Looking around, Claire saw nothing else on the street except warehouses.

Without anywhere or anyone else to turn to for help she just started limping fast down the street before erupting into a fledging but determined run. A run for her life.

* * *

While Claire was fleeing from the clutches of evil, Albert got out of his station wagon and strode down a quiet and desolate block in an industrial neighborhood in San Francisco, comprised mostly of drab colored warehouses and manufacturing plants. A few blocks to his right was the famous produce district, a couple of streets known for its companies that distributed fruits and veggies to destinations in the city as well as the rest of the Bay Area. In the meantime, his current destination was sandwiched between a compact indie shop that sold blown glass art and metal art and the offices of a printing press.

At first glance, the façade of Castle Blitzkrieg appeared nondescript and harmless enough, that is until you walked close enough to make out the image on the sign above the door, which included the same human skull wearing a Nazi-style, World War Two helmet that was on the front cover of the matchbook he'd found. A casual look at the menu was also suggestive enough, which included names of drinks like "The Fuhrer's Delight", "Genocide", "Goebbels's Goblet", and "The SS Mai Tai".

Deafening, vibrating death metal music slapped him right in the face as soon as he opened the heavy Gothic-style door, that could've easily been on any given street in Munich. It was semi-dark and hard to see inside the bar, which made it difficult to make out people's faces. But maybe they didn't want to be seen. Maybe that was the whole point. It was like being in a cave. A couple of the walls were adorned with Bauhaus art. Clusters of couples and groups were huddled together here and there, talking among themselves.

Albert felt eyes on him, on the back of his head specifically, as he drew closer to the bar, which was filled mostly with young people in Goth style clothing. Lots and lots of black and lots and lots of gaunt, pale faces. Maybe they were staring at him because he was old enough to be their uncle or father or because of the way he was dressed (dead giveaway to suburban dad or academic, scholarly type). *Or* perhaps it was because of…oh, he honestly didn't care one bit, quite frankly, why they were looking at him funny. Maybe they thought he was handsome or cute. He ought to tell that one to Claire sometime. She'd get a real kick out of that one, not to mention jealous, too.

The bartender, a guy with enough tattoos on his arms and neck to make him appear like Ray Bradbury's Illustrated Man, averted his eyes when Albert approached the bar, perhaps because the professor was the pink elephant in the room now.

Albert raised his voice amid the loud music. "Say, can I get an SS Mai Tai?" he asked.

The bartender nodded, neither his eyes nor his mouth smiling. Albert had encountered that many times before. He got the message loud and clear. The guy did make his drink promptly, he gave him that. Still, Albert pondered briefly if he should leave him a tip or not. *Remember, acknowledging him without being friendly or nice. I can play that game, too.* In the end he decided not to sweat over the trivial stuff, tossing a buck on the counter top. The bartender simply nodded at him again before attending to another customer.

Albert sauntered off to another part of the dimly lit bar, taking a sip of his drink and almost spat it back out immediately. *Jesus!* Talk about packing a wallop! This was probably the strongest Mai Tai he ever had. *Well, there's a reason why they named the drink, the SS Mai Tai. Probably potent enough to stop an elephant in its tracks.* Maybe the bartender was just trying to send him a message. Saying, *You're not welcome here!*

He walked over to a high table with a couple of stools around it, situated in the middle of the bar, and sat on one of the stools, observing all the action in the joint. As standoffish and hostile as this place was he had to admit it was still a good venue to people watch. He took it all in, trying to find any clues that may tell him where Claire might be, watching everything from the two Goth lovebirds sitting at a small, intimate corner table to his left, practically tasting the oozing, saccharine sweetness of their conversation, to the trio of hipster young men occupying a private booth, having a very animated discussion where they frequently used their hands to emphasize certain points.

Minutes later, when he wasn't receiving any luck from his surveillance he began feeling anxious and desperate, and strange thoughts popped up in his head about this environment and its patrons, thoughts that occasionally veered to the violent and dark. Irrational and outlandish thoughts that gave him a chill and shudder for even thinking about them. Like, for example, *The people in this bar are the epitome of disgusting, pathetic white trash and all of them deserve to die and they put all white people, good and bad, to ultimate shame...just look at them! None of these fucking losers have a future. Who are the parents and grandparents of these losers? They're the ones who instilled, taught, and planted all the racist and hateful seeds and ideas in their heads. Ideas like the holocaust never happened and that all Jews and people of color were to blame for the world's problems. The parents and grandparents ought to be killed, too! These people and others like them were responsible for Claire's disappearance. What the hell did they do with her?* If Albert had to shake the truth violently out of each and every one of them he would do it. He certainly wouldn't have a problem with that.

To prove that point, he almost got up from his stool and hurled his glass at the mirrored back wall of the bar, lined with bottles of booze of all different sizes, shapes, and colors. But his self-control kicked in immediately and saved his butt from the anger of the lynch mob and he refrained from what would have been such a foolish act that most definitely would have had consequences.

Then, almost ten minutes had passed before a tallish man with the blackest jet black hair he'd ever laid eyes on (appearing like ink), and dressed all in black, from head to toe, capped off by a long black trench coat. It looked like he could've had a shotgun, or a few shotguns, stowed away under that big trench coat. The tall man made a beeline straight to the bar without looking at anyone. He knew his business, his agenda, and made no bones about it. The bartender nodded at him and immediately poured him a shot of whiskey.

Obviously, they knew each other for the bartender already knew what his poison was before the man even uttered a single word. So the tall man was a regular here. A gnawing gut feeling prodded Albert the more he looked at him. There was something about this guy that captivated his attention, which kept his eyes fixated on him for some reason. Something about this dude screamed of white nationalism, more so than the dozen or so other folks in here. For Albert, it was the combination of the way he carried himself, his attitude, and also his sense of style, which was not that different from that of the other people here.

Which was precisely why Albert decided to follow him, discreetly of course, after the man gulped and downed his second shot of whiskey. He stood outside the bar's door and watched as the man dressed in black walked down the block and climbed into a big black sedan that was parked, ironically enough, in front of his station wagon. Albert looked down at his phone, trying to appear preoccupied, pretending that he was checking something, as the sedan drove by. The guy didn't seem to notice him. Albert strode quickly over to his station wagon, jumped in, and pursued him at a reasonably inconspicuous distance, allowing a couple of cars to serve as a buffer between them. If the guy was buzzed or drunk from all that booze he consumed he certainly didn't show it on the road, that's for sure. His sedan didn't swerve, fishtail, or veer off recklessly in different directions. So far, Albert as a true academic, graded him an A for his driving.

Traffic was fluid for the most part, with occasionally snags of bumper-to-bumper congestion here and there, as the black sedan guided him down Florida Street, one of many streets named after states in this part of town. After going through a consecutive series of green traffic lights, the sedan made a left turn, and a few minutes later, connected with Cesar Chavez Boulevard, a major thoroughfare that led them all the way down to a no-man's land kind of neighborhood of the city. The sort of neighborhood you wouldn't want your car to suddenly choke and break down in, day or night, and one replete with a huge landfill dump, an automobile junkyard stacked full of smashed and flattened cars that resembled crumpled sardine cans, and dozens of boarded up, graffiti festooned storefronts and abandoned vehicles. The kind of neighborhood ideal for dumping a corpse. The landfill would be perfect for that, Albert mused. He suddenly wondered if Claire was dead or not and immediately regretted thinking about that...no, she's just missing, that's all.

Now, no other motorists served as a cushion between his station wagon and the black sedan, but he still maintained a discreet and sizable distance behind the car. Once Albert drove past the landfill site he found himself on a desolate stretch of road that seemed to reach all the way to the waters of the bay. No one was walking on the streets here. No one was walking their dog in this neck of the woods. He sped past a weed-infested corner where an overturned mailbox lay on its side. As Albert kept driving on he saw nothing but neglected wasteland, dilapidated buildings, boarded-up homes, burned-out cars, and stray dogs running loose.

The bleak and dismal landscape continued for miles it seemed. The typically cheery and touristy picture-perfect San Francisco he knew so well, and the one that government and city officials wanted people to see, was all but gone from view. He was in a totally different world now. Not quite Third World country-ish but close. *Where the heck was this guy going to anyway?*

Then all of a sudden, as if his question was being answered by the heavens, he saw a lone figure straggling, and occasionally running in short bursts coming in his direction, along the side of the road. It wasn't until he got closer that his eyes widened and his jaw dropped open, for the person he saw shambling along like a zombie was none other than the one and only true love of his life, Claire. Her face was bruised and swollen like she was the loser of a major prize fight, discolored with hideous purple splotches that made them appear like they were birthmarks, with her bloodied left eye swollen shut. Dried blood was caked on to her left temple and the left side of her face, and some of it had dribbled down to her chin, from her cracked and split lips.

"Oh, my God!" he said, feeling like he would literally crumple over the steering wheel and die right there on the spot. He felt his heart sink. Before he could react in a timely manner the man in the black sedan beat him to the punch by pulling over to the shoulder of the road, jumping out of his car, and racing over to her rescue by trying to help her in the passenger seat of his vehicle as if he was some good Samaritan. When in fact he was probably the one who beat her up so bad in the first place.

Claire shoved him off of her with a look of pure rage on her face, pushed him pretty good, too, for the man almost lost his balance. But he nimbly maintained his stance, and being twice her size as well as two head lengths taller than her, he swooped his arms around her in a tight bear hug, trying to smother the life out of her. *And* trying to drag her into the car in the process.

Albert pulled over and immediately slammed on the brakes, bringing the station wagon to a screeching halt, as a cloud of dust pillowed up behind it. The man in black jerked his head in his direction, glaring at Albert as he leaped out of his car and tried to intervene.

"STOP!" the man bellowed. "Get back in your car and get the fuck out of here! Mind your own damn business!"

Claire shot Albert a weak and weary smile.

When Albert didn't budge, standing his ground, the man in black proceeded to try and shove her into his car. That's when Claire stomped his foot hard with the sharp heel of her boot and he winced in pain, his grip on her loosening. That was Albert's cue to dive right in, and he did so, by lunging at the guy, throwing his entire body at him, which was smaller in mass compared to the man's frame, but that strike totally threw the guy off guard, with Albert's forehead hammering his forehead and creating a sound like a dull clap. *Ouch! Boy, did that hurt!* But it was just the diversion he needed to stall and buy some time and distract the guy so his slimy hands would release Claire. Albert honestly didn't think he'd be able to get back up again, but lo and behold, he did. It was the tall man that actually seemed a little woozy and dazed as he tried to stand back up and find his balance. The look on the man's face was saying to him, "What the fuck?! Who the fuck are you, motherfucker?! How dare you barge in like this, sticking your nose in where it doesn't belong."

Without thinking, Albert jerked himself into action and brought his right arm up and sent his fist flying towards the man's face, where it connected by slamming full force into his left eye. The impact sounded like a quick pop. The man reeled backwards a little on unsteady feet. Albert took full advantage of the situation as the guy was trying to gather his composure, by delivering a series of punches to his face, with each one twisting his head left and right, back and forth, like he was reprimanding a child for naughty behavior.

A few seconds later, the man in black snapped back to attention in military-style mode, as if he was saluting the swastika, his face stone stoic, his two dark eyes glinting with pure hatred and hostility. With that motivation in hand, he leaped into a martial arts fighting stance and jumped at Albert, grabbing a hold of his torso, lifting him off the ground a little, and tried to flip him. A total *jiu-jitsu* move. When Albert resisted and struggled with him, trying to break out of the lock he had on him, the tall man applied more pressure and swiftly raised him off the floor before he could give him anymore problems, and deftly flipped him on his back. The next thing Albert knew he was staring up at the blue skies.

The tall man then got down on the ground and pin locked him with his legs, snatching Albert's left arm and twisted it, raising it up in the air, and trying to yank it in the direction away from his body. Albert cried in pain, immediately feeling the surge of electricity shooting through his nerves. The guy was trying to neutralize his opponent's abilities and tactics by turning them inwards towards Albert and not to him, the intended target. But before he could be one hundred percent successful in ripping Albert's arm out of its socket, Albert saw Claire sneak up behind the tall man and clobber him viciously in the head with a tire iron from Albert's station wagon. The tall man's pin lock on him loosened instantly like a trigger release and Albert was able to breathe once more. But he wasn't quite done just yet. When the tall man reached over and grabbed him again, this time with a seemingly unbreakable vise-lock grip, Claire raised that tire iron up in the air again and kept pounding it down on the man's face over and over again until it was nothing but a bloody red mush of brain matter, bone, and blood. Her hands, face, as well as her jacket, blouse, and skirt were all splattered with the guy's remains. Albert had to pull her off of the man because she wouldn't stop hammering him and he could feel the tremors in her body.

She kept shaking as she knelt there on the side of the road next to the guy, staring into space with that expression of *pure rage still etched on her face,* as if she was in trance mode, the tire iron still clutched in her bloody hands. He gently took the tool away from her. Her breaths coming out in short, hoarse bursts. It must be shock, Albert thought, quickly rushing over to her side and wrapping his arms around her protectively, stroking her back gently. She didn't seem to notice him at first, seemed oblivious to him, and didn't react to his touch, probably because the violent gravity of the incident was just beginning to sink in and had visibly jarred and traumatized her. And would continue to do so for the weeks and months to come.

A moment later, Claire rested her head against his shoulder as tears rolled down her cheeks.

He looked down at her and asked quietly, "Did he?"

She shook her head, not looking at him.

He sighed in relief, holding her firmly and giving her all the time and space in the world. She was going to need it.

CHAPTER THIRTEEN

"We'll claim it was self-defense," Albert suggested, standing at the side of Claire's hospital bed, gently caressing her soft and warm forearm. "He was going to kill me and during the heat of the moment you made an executive decision, because my life was in danger…and to save my life that's why you had to kill him. That's it."

She nodded, looking at him, finding it convincing enough. But jeez, movement of any kind, any kind whatsoever, was agonizing! It would re-trigger and emphasize the pain with a capital 'P' and she immediately would be aware and conscious of that splitting headache again. Even swallowing water was torture in itself. The meds they issued for the headache weren't helping. Claire came here at Albert's insistence. The truth of the matter was that she hated hospitals and avoided them if she could. To her they were evil corporations or institutions, similar to prisons, but not quite as bad as that. To her, they were places that were greedy and only cared about one thing. No, not the patient but *money*. She knew far too many women and rape victims who had bad experiences with hospitals, who wound up with the short end of the stick, so to speak, when it came down to whose side and story the hospitals chose to believe in. Those same women, those same victims, whose credibility seemed not to matter at all compared to that of the rapist. It was an unfair, unjust, upside down world indeed.

Claire could've taken care of herself at home. She knew enough and read enough about self-care to know what to do. But she was here now so thought she'd better make the best of it. When the nurse gave her the hand-held mirror the day she arrived and she saw her face in it, Claire almost dropped it. Initially, she couldn't believe that was her gazing back at herself in the mirror. It was like looking at another woman. All those swollen bruises and lacerations seemed to cover up the real her. It was like, *Is that really me??* Pretty jarring, in her opinion. Her swollen, puffy, and black-and-blue face. One eye bruised severely enough that she could hardly keep it open. It felt like she had a prosthetic appliance or mask over her face, like the kind you see actors wearing when they played the role of some fantastical creature or whatnot. After experiencing denial, anger and rage settled back in. Well, at least she had her vengeance. Still, when she thought of the man dressed in black her hands would curl up into tight fists and her heartbeat would accelerate. *Calm the fuck down!* she thought. *He's gone now. It's over. Don't blow out a blood vessel or artery over him. He's dead! Do you fucking hear me? Just think of his face that you bashed in.*

Albert's reassuring and loving touch pulled her out of her jungle of thoughts, out of her own little world, and back into the here and now. She moistened her dry, cracked lips with her tongue, feeling her throat get itchy and parched like sandpaper. Her lips were so cracked and split that she tasted the coppery, metallic residue of blood on them. She reached over to a glass of water on the tray before her and took a few swallows. Much, much better.

"I have a few good lawyer friends," Albert continued. "I've already talked to them and they said they can help us. They want to hear what you have to say."

She nodded again, wincing when she felt the headache. It would be best to listen to him. It felt good to be supported and to have someone in your corner and to have someone else take charge and make decisions for a change.

He saw the expression on her face when she nodded. "Still painful, huh?" he asked softly, grabbing her hand and squeezing it gently.

"Yes," she replied quietly.

"Want me to ask the nurse for some more tablets?"

"No, it's okay," she answered, neglecting to tell him the meds weren't helping her at all.

"The doctors said they scheduled some tests for your head and brain to see if there is any damage or trauma to it," Albert added.

"Okay," Claire replied in the same tone of voice. A sudden thought popped up in her head. "What day is it?"

"Tuesday."

She shifted slightly in the bed, lifting the blanket gingerly so as to not provoke or aggravate the headache and pain in her body, and slowly began swinging her legs towards the edge of the mattress. "I need to prep for my Wednesday classes. And I need to get back to the volunteers who attended the recent orientation training...have to inform them about the follow up training as well as distribute the new volunteer handbooks."

"Whoa, whoa! Oh, no you don't!" he smiled, gently grabbing a hold of her shoulders and pushing her back down into bed. "Miss Busy Body you aren't! At least not for a while. You need to rest and recuperate, babe. Doctor's orders and mine as well."

"But...but I've got so much to do," Claire persisted.

"And you'll have adequate time to get it all done *after* you heal," he replied gently. "Okay?"

She was silent for a moment, not looking at him, but eventually nodded her head slowly. "How long do I have to stay here?"

"That's what we're waiting to hear back about from your doctor." He glanced at his watch. "Said she'd get back to us by four today. Lift your head, babe." She obeyed and he grabbed her pillow, fluffed and fattened it up, and reinserted it under her head. She lied back down. "There, nice and comfy. Cozy, huh? In the meantime, rest up, eat and enjoy this bland hospital food as best as you can, and if you need anything give me a holler. Okay?"

Claire grabbed his wrist. "Wait, don't go!"

He squeezed her hand, shooting her the most reassuring and charming smile he could muster. Oh, God, she loved his smile! Her heart swooned and melted immediately upon seeing it. That grin could remedy and fix the crappiest day she'd ever experienced and make things better all over again, lifting her spirits. Enough said. It was priceless. And it was a sure fire reminder of why and how she fell in love with him all those years ago back in New York City. Another lifetime ago it seemed.

"I'm not going anywhere, sweetie," he consoled her. "I'm staying put, right here, right next to you." Stabbing his finger down at the floor, for extra emphasis, when he said, "I'm staying put, right here."

That made her feel like she was up on a pedestal all by herself, like a goddess, like she mattered and meant something to him.

"*And*, as you can see," Albert added, gesturing with a generous sweep of his arm at the little collection of personal items gathered on a comfortable looking fabric chair that the nurses probably supplied him with. These items included such essential, everyday things as a day bag, a backpack, a pillow, lap blanket, laptop, and a stack of well-thumbed and trusty books. The books were definitely a requirement for a college professor. "Since I'll be staying here for the long haul, during visiting hours, I might as well make myself comfortable and useful, right?"

Claire beamed at him. "Yep! You've got the perfect attitude."

He remained at her side, stroking her arm. "Hey, you want anything, hon? Some juice perhaps? A little chocolate maybe? Name your guilty pleasure and if old Albert doesn't have it I'll run and get it for you."

She nodded eagerly, maybe *too* enthusiastically, hitting a button on the hospital bed console so it reclined into a sitting position. "Chocolate!"

Albert grinned. "Knew that would hook you, line and sinker. It had to! It's one of your favorite things." He walked over to the day bag, fished out a candy bar from it, and began peeling it open. Then he handed it to her, who happily accepted it from him, gleeful smiles and all.

Her eyes widened. "*Oooooooooh*, it's my favorite brand, too!" Breaking off a piece of the bar and munching on it.

Albert shot her that 'all knowing' look, to show her he wasn't born yesterday. "Hey, c'mon now, I *know* all your favorites."

"Let's share," she said, snapping off another chunk from the bar and offering it to him.

"Aw, you're so sweet," he replied, claiming the piece from her.

Claire grinned mischievously, narrowing her eyes to slits. "A whole lot sweeter than this candy I bet."

"*Uhm-hmmm.*"

She nodded at his stuff near the chair, helping herself to another offering of chocolate. "Whatcha gonna work on?"

"For starters, finish reading and grading the essays from my afternoon anthro class. Boy, I have to tell you, some of these kids really know their stuff and don't mess around. They know how tough and challenging it is to be at a school like Cal, much like our mentality was when we were at Columbia. They know it's the survival of the fittest and that only the strong survive. They know it's the *real* deal."

She nodded, tilting her head a little like she always did when she was checking in with him. "You're proud of them, aren't you?"

"I am. At the fact that they are giving it their all and striving to be the cream of the crop. Hey, we're talking about our future leaders, scientists, teachers, educators, and politicians here, you know."

"Respecting the future generation," Claire added. "Yeah, I see that in some of the students in the women's studies program, too. Quite a number of them have that firebrand, radical feminist energy to be the next revolutionaries in the field."

"Speaking of firebrand, I think you'd better extinguish your own flame and get some much needed shut eye and rest," he advised. "What cha say, babe?"

"Okay. Let's talk more later." She clicked a button on the console and the overhead light went off.

He brought the blanket up close to her chin, tucking it in like he was doing it for a child. Then he ruffled her dark brown hair and bent down to kiss her.

"Read me a bedtime story?" she teased.

"Next time," he whispered, kissing her again.

He stepped over to the chair and sat down, making himself comfortable, crossing his legs. She watched for a bit as he took out a pen and began the arduous task of plucking that first essay from a mountainous, intimidating stack of papers and reading it, writing comments on the side margins as he went along. Claire was well familiar with that duty. An expression of deep set concentration was etched on his face. She looked on for a little more, wondering what he was thinking about as he was working, before her eyelids began feeling heavy, as if stones were sitting on them. After yawning a couple of times, she finally closed her eyes, turning to her side a little, and succumbed to sleep moments later.

When she woke up later, sometime around ten thirty that night, she turned her head and saw that Albert and his collection of stuff were gone. The chair empty. She sat up bolt upright in the bed, eyes wide open, clutching onto the blanket, her heart fluttering a little, and feeling a queasy, anxious sensation in the pit of her stomach. *Did visiting hours end already?* she wondered. *That was fast.* When she turned her head back to the tray in front of her she saw a sheet of paper lying there that she didn't see before, folded in half. She turned on the light, picked up the paper, opened it, and read the message inside: 'You were resting and sleeping beautifully when visiting hours ended and I didn't want to wake you. I spoke with your doctor and she said that they'd like to keep you for one more day of observation and testing. I'll be back in the morning. See you soon.

Love always,

Albert'

Claire read the note a second time before putting it back on the tray. *I wish he would have awakened me.* It would have been nice to see that smile of his before he left. She ran her tongue over her dry lips again and then turned to her left and reached over to her purse which was sitting on the nightstand next to the bed. After rummaging through her purse, she found what she was searching for. *Ah-hah!* That elusive chapstick. She applied some on her lips. Claire then plucked her phone out of her purse, checking to see if she received any text messages. Several. Two of them were from Albert. And one voicemail from her parents. She found her mother's phone number, punching the **Call** button. She loved her mother to death (and her father, too.) but realized, as she often did when communicating with her, that she was a worry wart who freaked out and stressed out over every little thing and detail in life. Nagging and reminding her about this, that, and the other. Even though Claire was forty-two years old! *Good Lord!* Claire kept her phone pressed to her left ear, closed her eyes for a moment, and simply allowed her mother to go on auto-pilot for about two minutes or so straight without stopping. When her mom was finished speaking, Claire acknowledged her comments and kept saying, "Yes, yes, yes," or "Okay, okay," told her mother that she loved her and her father very much, and then hung up.

After putting her phone away, she turned off the overhead light, and snuggled up under the blanket.

Before she was about to turn on her side and shut her eyes, a nurse with a friendly grin stepped into the room. "You doing okay?" she asked.

"Yes," Claire replied.

"Need anything before I go on my break?"

"No, I'm fine. Thank you."

"Just press the button if you want something."

"I will. Thanks."

And the nurse was gone.

Claire closed her eyes and shortly after that, much to her surprise and without any difficulty, fell into a restful slumber. She slept solidly like a log in her warm cocoon until midway through the night, when she heard the dull squeak of the hospital room's door opening slowly. *Oh, it's just the nurse,* she thought.

When she opened her eyes, expecting to see that nurse with a friendly grin standing there, Claire's eyes widened like saucers, and she shrank back in the bed, when she saw a young white man instead. And no, he was not a male nurse for he was *not* wearing a nurse's uniform. Rather, he was dressed in a preppyish, beige three-piece suit, with a bright and vivid turquoise tie nestled between the collars of his crisp white sleeve shirt. His blonde hair, long on the top and short on the sides, was one of the main things that stood out about him. Yes, the "Fashy Haircut". She was all too familiar with that term when doing her research and writing of her controversial book on the white nationalist movement. The young man who stared at her now was also a familiar face.

"You're *not* allowed in here!" Claire said. "How'd you get in here?"

The young man shot her a wicked grin. "Oh, I have my ways."

"Get the hell out!"

The man didn't budge an inch. Instead, after allowing a profound moment to pass, one in which he basically told her he didn't take any frickin' orders from her, he approached her bedside with a suave saunter. It had a bit of a funky swagger to it, like he was Mister Pimp Daddy, full of arrogance and cockiness. Claire recoiled back from him even further, stretching back in the bed as far as she could go, like she would from a king cobra snake.

The young man stopped abruptly in front of the bed just as he was exactly an inch away from it, and not a hair further than that. Then he had the gutsy balls, the sheer audacity, to lean his face in so close to hers that she could literally smell his stinky aftershave as well as his breath that reeked of coffee.

He glared directly in her eyes. "You and I both know well in our hearts, in our brains, and in our blood, what you did. The sin *you* committed recently. *You killed a man. Shame on you.*"

She was momentarily paralyzed by an electric current of guilt that rippled throughout her body, too stunned to speak or react, simply staring back at him with her mouth hanging open, seeing that lethal venom in his eyes. He had basically just awakened her with a mind-numbing reality check without actually grabbing her shoulders and throttling her about it. His chilling words really hit home for her and she felt it deep down in her bones, in her marrow, and in her bowels, eating and grinding her from the inside out. Yes, she had killed someone…there was no denying or erasing that fact. It couldn't be sugar-coated or reinterpreted another way. She could not go back in time to change it. That was impossible. The sheer gravity of what she did...it was difficult for her to wrap her head around it sometimes...difficult for her to fathom. On some days she'd wake up in the morning and suddenly think to herself, *Oh, God, I killed someone!* And all the self-defense excuses she had stockpiled in her head, all the anti-rape training that was stored in the database of her brain, simply flew out the window.

Keeping his face perfectly still, he added with the same chill in his tone of voice, "And the man you killed was my *friend*." Trying to make her feel even guiltier.

"Well, you sure got a lousy taste in friends!" she fired back. "Do they all enjoy slapping and beating women around?"

With his face so close to hers, Claire felt the palpable tension and hostility emanating from his body, so thick that she thought it would literally strangle her...so close to her that she could feel the heat coming from his breath. They were almost nose to nose now and it was probably his way of showing her that he was not afraid of her one bit.

"Only to those that threaten, intimidate, and bully organizations like mine," he hissed, his blue eyes appearing more and more like those of a snake. "That jeopardizes my organization's mission and goals...we can't have you spreading any more lies and rumors about us, Miss Goldman. That ends now. If only you had been wise enough not to have written that book of yours, all would've been well.

But no, it was your way or the highway. How unfortunate for you."

And that was when he thrust his arms forward and grabbed her throat, squeezing it tightly. When he applied more pressure she began gasping for air, trying to shove him off of her but having very little success at that. Claire kept sucking for air, choking, feeling like she was engaged in the swimming component of a triathlon, her hands pushing on his chest in a seemingly futile effort to stop him. The harder he squeezed, the less force she was able to exert. This see-saw battle continued for a few moments longer before she was slammed back against the bed, shaking it violently, as she tried to reinforce and maintain her hands on his chest. But the man kept bearing his weight down on her, driving himself forward with such fierce determination and relentlessness for a person not that big in mass and size, certainly not as big as the man in black was. A maniacal, twisted look was etched on his face as he continued pushing, squeezing with all his might it seemed, for she felt his fingernails penetrating and slicing into the skin of her neck.

Claire started choking again, gasping for air, feeling lightheaded all of a sudden, feeling like she was drowning, as the flow of oxygen to her brain was temporarily obstructed. *Fight!* she commanded herself. *Fight back now! C'mon, woman! Don't give up on me just yet...you got this!*

A brilliant idea suddenly popped up in her head and she spat in his face with as much venom and rage as she could muster, causing his grip on her neck to loosen just a tad. But that was enough…enough for her to stab him swiftly in the eyes with her fingers, sending him reeling backwards as he clutched his eyes protectively, yelping like an injured dog. More importantly, it also gave her an opportune amount of precious time to snatch up her purse, reach in, and pluck out a tiny black bottle.

After the young man had regained his composure, he turned towards her and lunged. But Claire already had the black bottle at the ready in her hand, aimed carefully, and fired, shooting a lethal amount of mace at the man's face. He screamed, his hands immediately gripping his face, trying to claw and wipe away the chemicals out of his eyes, nose, and mouth. But she kept spraying it at him, dousing him generously with it like it was lighter fluid being used at a summertime barbeque.

The man kept screaming, spinning around like a top. "You fucking bitch! I can't see! I can't see anymore!"

She almost responded by saying, 'That's the whole point, you dumbass!' but refrained.

He eventually lost his balance on the slippery floor, clumsily tripping on his own feet and collapsed to the ground, rubbing the liquid away from his eyes with the sleeves of his coat now. Suddenly, the door of the hospital room flung open and the nurse with the friendly grin (although she was not smiling at the moment) ran in, her eyes bulging at what she saw. And not seeming to believe any bit of the craziness she was staring at, judging by the jaw dropping expression on her face.

Claire, panic-stricken, gazed at her desperately. "Please call security!" she said.

* * *

They took a long walk together.

And it was a much, much needed one, too, for they had been pretty much holed up in the house for a good part of the weekend and they were both desperate to get some fresh air as well as some exercise in. She felt lethargic, her back and shoulders were as stiff as a board, her brain processing speeds and reflexes sluggish and delayed from sitting too much and looking at screens (not to mention giving her bad posture from being hunched over her computer), and she kept yawning and yawning (*what the devil is that all about?*), which was just so uncharacteristic of how she usually was. Usually she was the complete opposite of how she felt now: active with a spring to her step, full of pep, zest, and energy along with a head full of questions and an inquisitive curiosity about the world. Well, all that was out the window at the current moment.

The duration of the walk was mostly in silence. But she didn't mind that for it allowed her time to think. Because her mind felt like a war zone after all she had been through lately...explosions, bombardments, loud, deafening noises, people screaming and yelling in her ear, and her body being thrashed around like it weighed nothing at all. She needed a time out, a respite to decompress and process everything, and she had been doing exactly that this weekend. Now, what she would really like, and maybe she'd have some time later to do this, was to go on a nice, long, sweaty run, get some cardio in and get her heart pumping again and get those endorphins to kick in. And throw in lifting some weights as well. Yeah, that's what she really wanted. Right now her body felt out of shape and her mind didn't feel as razor sharp as it typically was, sharp to the point where she could tackle and deal with anything at all.

But the walk definitely helped. It was a start, at least, and something to build on. One thing she noticed during the walk was the absence of anger and rage in her mind. Hot, boiling, white knuckle rage at those two men who tried to kill her. Now truth be told, the anger wasn't completely and totally gone, of course, but rather it had subsided and cooled off in a lower and hidden recess of her brain. To erupt and explode later on. That would be the pattern of her trauma for God knows how many weeks, months, or years. Hard to say, really, at this point. Maybe she'd learn to suck it up with her chin up and deal with it. That's what most people usually did anyway. Or maybe she would need therapy. It wouldn't be the first time for that.

As they walked, she'd hold Albert's hand occasionally. Other times she wouldn't. The majority of the time she was close to his side and liked having him close in proximity, in case anything happened, but also relished independence and standing on her own two feet. She knew that *if* she was faced with being alone, including being single, she could do it. But that was not Claire's choice right now. Right now she wanted Albert in her life and did not wish to be alone. Solitude would not be a healthy option, mentally and physically, for her right now because of what she had gone through. She welcomed all the support, friendship, and love she could get.

Claire reached out and grabbed a hold of Albert's hand again, squeezing it tight, turning and studying the rather introspective expression on his face. "Whatcha thinking about?" she asked quietly.

"Memories mostly," he replied, looking down at the sidewalk as they walked.

Now her curiosity was piqued. Claire looked at him, tilting her head a little as she checked in with him. "*Oh?* Which ones?"

"Like that time we went to your apartment right after class ended and it was raining so hard that it was coming down in sheets. Big, fat raindrops, too."

Claire nodded, her recall of that day still quite vivid surprisingly. "Oh, yeah, I remember that."

"Do you remember stripping off all your wet and soggy clothes the moment you set foot in your unit? And that after cranking up the heater you threw on that thick purple bathrobe I gave you for Christmas and padded barefoot into the kitchen and made us kosher baloney and cheese sandwiches for dinner?"

She paused as her brain tried to access that part of the memory, one from a quarter of a century ago. "Yes," she finally answered, elbowing him playfully in the ribs with a shake of her head. "I bet I know why you remember that part so well. You have such a one-track mind."

Albert chuckled. "No, I was going to say those sandwiches you made were so yummy! I'm salivating thinking about them now."

"They were just ordinary baloney sandwiches," she replied, saying it in such a way to imply that they weren't anything special or unique. At least not to her anyway, having grown up in a household where dishes like that were very common and frequent.

"Can you make me a sandwich like that again?" he inquired innocently, like a child requesting a special treat.

Now it was her turn to laugh. *"Seriously? That's what college students eat. I thought you're into more sophisticated foodie fare nowadays."*

"A pretentious food snob critic I'm not. No, no, no, that's what I want! That sandwich. My guilty pleasures are simple. C'mon, you know that."

Claire chuckled. "Okay, okay. If that's the last meal you want on this planet you shall receive it, hon."

"Oh, since you put it that way let me see what else I can add to the menu." He looked up from the sidewalk. "Can I add spinach lasagna to my order?"

Claire smirked. "Okay. Anything else?"

Albert hesitated for just a brief moment, thinking. "No, that's it."

Maybe he didn't want to overstay his welcome by asking or demanding too much from her.

"Any other memories?" she asked curiously.

His face lit up with a grin. "Remember our Vegas honeymoon?"

She rolled her eyes with a groan. "How can I forget it? The sauna in the hotel room with the yucky strands of hair from past guests? And need I remind you about the sticky, grimy carpet and the cum stained bedsheets?"

"The trip wasn't all bad."

She softened up a little, nodding. "True. The best and most grand buffet to end all buffets...had one of the best massages of my life on that trip. As well as one of the best nights out on the town, culminating at that techno nightclub."

"Fun times?"

She nodded with a smile, thinking about it. "Yeah, I'd say so...what brought back these memories anyway?"

He shrugged. "They just organically came to me, is all."

They approached the next intersection, a small, quiet one with a corner liquor store and a deli and a laundry mat. A few children were playing hopscotch on the sidewalk outside the laundry mat, probably waiting with their parents as their clothes dried.

"So you want to have this special meal today I presume?" she asked.

"Would that be too much trouble for you?" he asked sheepishly.

She shook her head. "No. Let's stop by the store to grab some stuff. Sound good?"

"Yes, it does." He smiled. "This will be fun. It'll be like old times."

Claire grinned, too. "Please step into my time machine," she replied, using her right hand to open an imaginary door for him.

Albert played along with her, pretending to climb into the machine.

She raised her index finger. "Wait, one thing, though! Are you sure you want to be with me? I tend to attract trouble from the controversy I stir up."

"I'm going to ignore that question," he replied.

She looked directly in his eyes and saw the true love burning in them, like coals of fire. Claire smiled, got into the imaginary driver's seat, and said, "Let's go."

THE END

BIOGRAPHY

Derek Muk is a writer and social worker from California. His short stories have appeared in various small press/indie magazines, including: New Realm, Cheapjack Pulp, Ink Stains Anthology, Nebula Rift, 9 Tales, Story of the Month Club, Fiction On The Web, Whispers From The Past: Fright and Fear (anthology), Dark Eclipse, The Dead Walk (anthology), 13 Magazine, Diabolic Tales 3, Both Barrels of Legends of the Monster Hunter I and II, The Trigger Reflex: Legends of the Monster Hunter II (anthology), Suffer the Little Children (anthology), Splatter: An Anthology of Horror, Death Rattle, Dark Things II (Anthology), Anthology of Ichor: Hearts of Darkness, Twisted Tongue Magazine, Static Movement, Sex and Murder Magazine, Sinister Tales, Night to Dawn, M-Brane SF, Sonar4 E-Zine, The Ethereal Gazette, 7th Dimension Magazine, Switchblade Magazine, ESC! Magazine, Scorched Wings Magazine, Hardboiled, Masque Noir, Detective Mystery Stories, Dawnsky, The Pinehurst Journal, Mystery Forum Magazine, The Green Queen, Kracked Mirror Mysteries, Golden Visions Magazine, Crossroads Magic, The Street Corner Magazine, Calliope Magazine, Unspoken Water, Space and Time Magazine, Infernal Ink Magazine, Tales of the Talisman Magazine, Aurora Wolf, The Horror Zine Magazine, Disturbed Digest, and Parabnormal Digest.

His novellas include *Being Followed* (published by DEMAIN), *Private Number/Claws* (published by Unnerving), *The Haunted Academy* (published by Midnight Frost Books), *The Demon Seeds* (published by Black Bedsheet Books), and *The Hanging Man* (published by Gloom House Publishing). His two chapbooks include: *Three Parts* and *Sin After Sin*.

His other published work includes: *The Occult Files of Albert Taylor* (a short story collection).

In addition to writing, he enjoys reading, going to bookstores, traveling, museums, art, dining out, and meeting new people. He has a Bachelor's and Master's degree in social work.

Visit his author website at:
http://theoccultfilesofalberttaylor.wordpress.com/

ADRIAN BALDWIN (COVER DESIGNER)

WINNER of INDIE NOVEL OF THE YEAR 2016 (Readers' Choice) at Underground Book Reviews

Adrian Baldwin is a Mancunian now living and working in Wales. Back in the Nineties, he wrote for various TV shows/personalities: Smith & Jones, Clive Anderson, Brian Conley, Paul McKenna, Hale & Pace, Rory Bremner (and a few others). Wooo, get him.

Since then, he has written three screenplays, one of which received generous financial backing from the Film Agency for Wales. Then along came the global recession to kick the UK Film industry in the nuts. What a bummer!

Not to be outdone, he turned to novel writing - which had always been his real dream - and in particular, a genre he feels is often overlooked; a genre he has always been a fan of: Dark Comedy (sometimes referred to as Horror's weird cousin).

BARNACLE BRAT (a dark comedy for grown-ups), his first novel won Indie Novel of the Year 2016 award (see above) - his second novel STANLEY McCLOUD MUST DIE! (More dark comedy for grown-ups) published in 2016, and his third novel: THE SNOWMAN AND THE SCARECROW (another dark comedy for grown-ups) published in 2018.

Adrian Baldwin has also written several dark comedy short stories, some of which he has published himself, whilst others have appeared in anthologies published by a variety of indie publishers.

His latest project, DEVIL'S ACRE, is a horror/sci-fi/period drama; it's basically Victorians vs 'aliens' vs zombies! What's not to like. The unfolding story will be released in a series of novellas/novelettes – with Episode 1 The Great Stink already out there.

Adrian cites his major influences as Kurt Vonnegut, Monty Python, Stephen King, David Bowie, Christopher Moore, David Mitchell, Robert Rankin, Galton & Simpson, Colin Bateman, Bruce Robinson, Jasper Fforde and Irvine Welsh.

For more information on the award-winning author, check out: www.adrianbaldwin.info (*You can read the beginnings of all his works there.)

DEMAIN PUBLISHING

To keep up to-date on all news DEMAIN (including future submission calls and releases) you can follow us in a number of ways:

BLOG:
www.demainpublishingblog.weebly.com

TWITTER:
@DemainPubUk

FACEBOOK PAGE:
Demain Publishing

INSTAGRAM:
demainpublishing